THE PROFIT SUTRAS-CHANAKYA'S WISDOM FOR MODERN ENTREPRENEURS

IMPROVE CASH FLOW, GROW PROFITS, AND LEAD YOUR BUSINESS WITH CLARITY

BRIJESH PARIKH

Copyright © Brijesh Parikh
All Rights Reserved.

This book has been self-published with all reasonable efforts taken to make the material error-free by the author. No part of this book shall be used, reproduced in any manner whatsoever without written permission from the author, except in the case of brief quotations embodied in critical articles and reviews.

The Author of this book is solely responsible and liable for its content including but not limited to the views, representations, descriptions, statements, information, opinions and references ["Content"]. The Content of this book shall not constitute or be construed or deemed to reflect the opinion or expression of the Publisher or Editor. Neither the Publisher nor Editor endorse or approve the Content of this book or guarantee the reliability, accuracy or completeness of the Content published herein and do not make any representations or warranties of any kind, express or implied, including but not limited to the implied warranties of merchantability, fitness for a particular purpose. The Publisher and Editor shall not be liable whatsoever for any errors, omissions, whether such errors or omissions result from negligence, accident, or any other cause or claims for loss or damages of any kind, including without limitation, indirect or consequential loss or damage arising out of use, inability to use, or about the reliability, accuracy or sufficiency of the information contained in this book.

Made with ♥ on the Notion Press Platform
www.notionpress.com

To every **entrepreneur**
who dares to build not just a business,
but a life of purpose and peace—
this book is for you.

To **Acharya Chanakya**,
whose ancient insights continue to guide
modern minds toward financial wisdom.

And most of all,
to my unwavering support system—
Trupti, my wife and true partner in every step,
Shiven and **Shachi**, my greatest sources of inspiration.
You are the why behind everything I do.

With love, purpose, and deep gratitude.

Contents

Contents

Contents

Contents

Preface

Every business begins with hope—
to serve, to grow, and to build something meaningful.
Yet too many entrepreneurs find themselves trapped by the very thing they set out to master: money.

As a financial planner, advisor, and student of timeless strategy, I've witnessed two things repeatedly:

The most brilliant business owners often put themselves last.

Ancient Indian wisdom holds solutions modern systems are only just discovering.

This book was born from a deep desire to bridge these worlds.

On one side: **Chanakya**, the revered strategist and economist, whose sutras have guided kings, empires, and thinkers for over two millennia.

On the other: the **Profit First methodology by** Mike Michalowicz—a proven, modern approach to business cashflow that empowers entrepreneurs to pay themselves first, build lasting reserves, and run lean, focused operations.

Through this book, I have reinterpreted 24 of Chanakya's most powerful financial and governance principles through the lens of the **Profit Maximiser system**—a "Provide Yourself First" cashflow model designed specifically for Indian business owners and professionals.

Each chapter is not just a lesson, but a call to action.
To run your business with clarity.
To serve your vision without sacrificing yourself.
To profit with purpose—and peace.

If you're ready to reclaim control of your money, your business, and your legacy, this book is your guide.

With gratitude,

Brijesh Parikh,CWM®

SEBI Registered Investment Advisor

Founder, Planet Wealth

Acknowledgements

This book is the result of not just my own ideas, but of the wisdom, encouragement, and quiet support of many people who walked alongside me on this journey.

First and foremost, to **Trupti**, my wife—your unwavering faith, patience, and presence have been the foundation upon which this work stands. To **Shiven** and **Shachi**, your energy and curiosity remind me every day why building something meaningful matters.

To my clients and fellow entrepreneurs—your challenges, conversations, and victories have shaped the real-world relevance of this book. Thank you for trusting me with your financial journeys and inspiring me to simplify wealth for all.

To **Mike Michalowicz**, whose groundbreaking work Profit First has empowered countless business owners to rethink money management—thank you for bringing structure and sanity into the world of entrepreneurship. Your influence is woven throughout these pages.

To the ancient genius of **Acharya Chanakya**, whose sutras continue to guide strategy, finance, and human behavior thousands of years later—your timeless relevance is the soul of this book.

To my **BNI network** and my **chapter PETRA** , thank you for being a constant source of ideas, encouragement, and accountability. The vision for the Profit Maximiser coaching and consulting framework was born through countless conversations, connections, and shared belief in adding value. You've inspired not only this book—but the movement behind it.

To my team at Planet Wealth, your belief in the mission of financial clarity and empowerment has been the wind beneath this project.

And finally, to every reader who chooses this book—I honor your commitment to growth, both personal and financial.

Thank you,
Brijesh Parikh

Prologue

In every era, in every culture, wealth has played two roles—one as a tool of empowerment, and the other as a source of struggle.

The entrepreneur of today is no different from the leader of ancient times. The battlefield may have changed—from royal courts to boardrooms, from handwritten scrolls to spreadsheets—but the questions remain timeless:

How do I build wealth that lasts?

How do I avoid burnout while growing my business?

How do I lead with purpose, and not just pressure?

In ancient India, one man understood this balance better than most. Acharya Chanakya, the mastermind behind the Mauryan Empire, believed that strong leadership and wise financial management were inseparable. His sutras were more than political counsel—they were timeless laws of economics, governance, and self-discipline.

Fast-forward to today, where despite technological advancement and financial tools, entrepreneurs still find themselves trapped in the same loop: generating revenue without retaining profit, sacrificing personal wellbeing at the altar of business growth, and serving others while ignoring themselves.

That's where this book finds its purpose.

The Profit Sutras is more than a blend of ancient philosophy and modern financial tools. It's a declaration—that you deserve to profit, that you must provide for yourself first, and that business is not just about numbers, but about dharma.

By combining Chanakya's wisdom with the Profit Maximiser system—a contemporary, actionable cashflow management framework—you'll learn not only how to grow your business, but how to grow with it.

This book is not a lecture. It is a journey. A roadmap for those who seek wealth, not just in numbers, but in freedom, clarity, and legacy.

As you turn the pages, I invite you to not just read—but to act.

To reclaim control of your business.

To restore your relationship with money.

And to lead, as Chanakya once taught, from a position of inner strength and outer clarity.

Welcome to the path.

Your profit is not the end—it is your beginning.

Common Mistakes to Avoid While Managing Business Cashflow Profitably

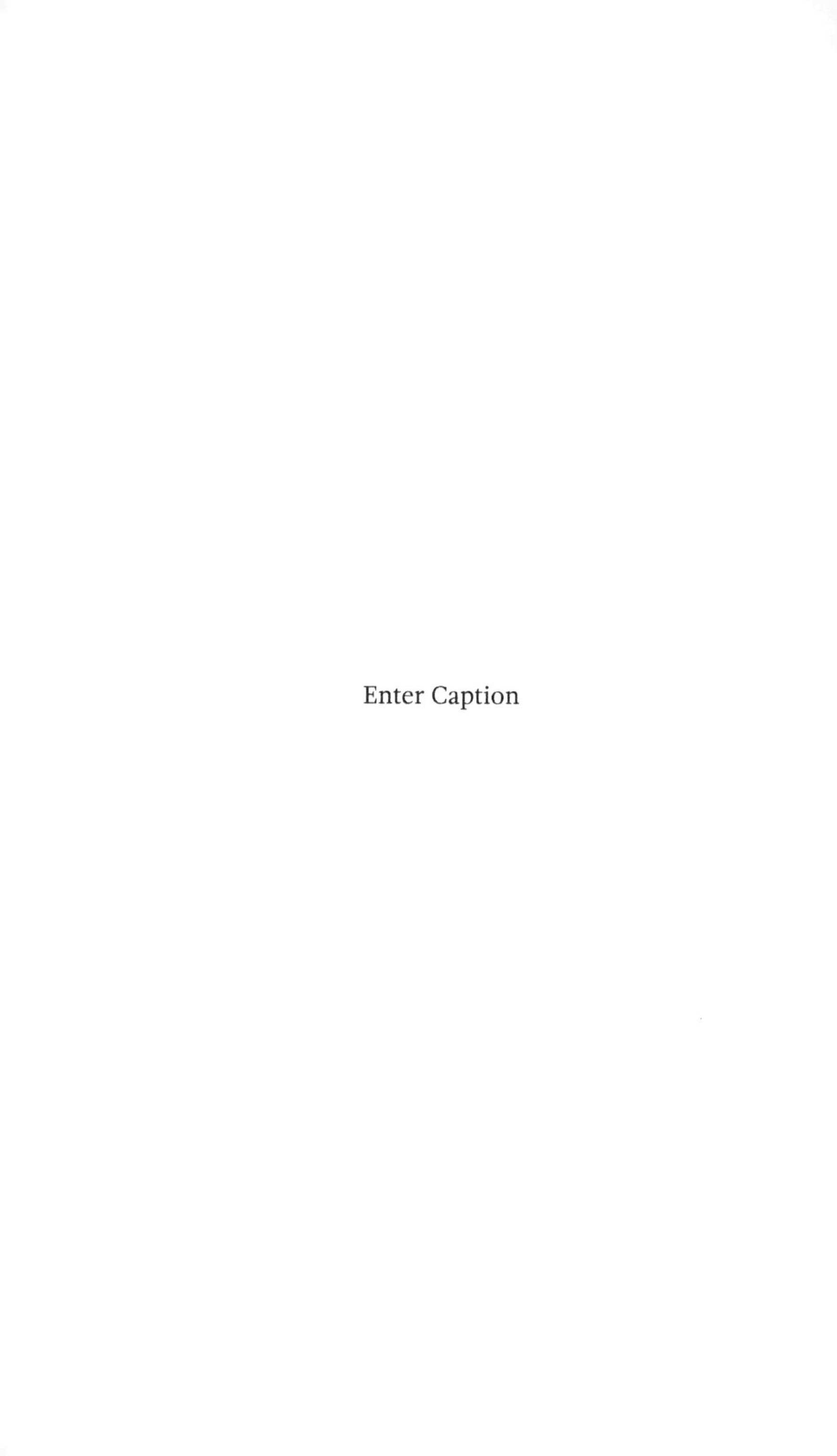

Enter Caption

CHAPTER ONE

Provide Yourself First – A Timeless Principle Reimagined for Modern Business

In every era, across every culture, there exists a silent struggle for those who build empires—whether of stone or strategy, brick or business: the struggle to grow wealth without losing peace, to create value without collapsing from pressure, and to serve the world without sacrificing oneself.

Modern entrepreneurs often find themselves last in line:

- Paying vendors before paying themselves.
- Running operations with no reserves.
- Living month-to-month despite growing revenue.
- Feeling trapped in a business meant to bring freedom.

But what if the solution wasn't new? What if it was hidden in the wisdom of the ancients? What if a 2,300-year-old teacher had already mapped the way?

That teacher was Chanakya—India's greatest political strategist, economist, philosopher, and royal advisor.

The Ancient Root: Chanakya and Self-Preservation Before Service

Chanakya understood that no kingdom could survive if the king was weak, broke, or directionless. He consistently advocated:

- Strong internal reserves before external commitments.
- Personal well-being of the leader before the needs of the state.
- Preservation of treasury before generous spending.

He taught kings: *You must protect your throne first, or there will be no kingdom to serve.*

This wisdom mirrors what we now know in business as the Profit First philosophy.

The Modern Evolution: Profit First Becomes "Provide Yourself First"

Popularized by Mike Michalowicz, the Profit First system flips conventional accounting:

Revenue – Expenses = Profit becomes Revenue – Profit = Expenses.

It demands that the business owner allocate a portion of every rupee earned to Profit, Taxes, and Owner's Pay—before spending on operating expenses.

The philosophy is simple: You must provide for yourself first.

But herein lies the breakthrough: this isn't a new idea. It's a principle that *Chanakya taught centuries ago*. He just used different words.

The Integration: Where East Meets Execution

This book unites two worlds:

1. Chanakya's timeless sutras – drawn from the Arthashastra and interpreted for entrepreneurs.
2. The Profit Maximiser system – a cash flow management model adapted from Profit First, made actionable for Indian businesses.

Each chapter is structured around one Chanakyan sutra and paired with:

- Its relevance to wealth and business.
- A Profit Maximiser application.
- Actionable steps for modern implementation.
- A real-world business case study.

You'll learn how ancient wisdom can:

- Help you grow wealth with structure, not stress.
- Build discipline without rigidity.
- Protect reserves from market swings and emotional spending.
- Create a business that rewards you—not one that runs you.

Why "Provide Yourself First" Isn't Selfish—It's Strategic

Too many business owners confuse sacrifice with leadership. But your business cannot be generous if it is gasping. You cannot uplift others if you are barely surviving.

Providing for yourself first:

- Creates stability.
- Builds confidence.
- Reduces dependence on debt.
- Models financial wisdom for your team and community.

It's not about greed. It's about governance.

As Chanakya might say: "Only the king with a filled treasury can withstand the siege."

What This Book Will Do for You

By the end of this book, you will:

- Have a step-by-step system to manage business finances.
- Build consistent, growing profits—even from irregular income.
- Pay yourself regularly without guilt.
- Fund taxes, growth, and impact without stress.
- Anchor your financial decisions in 2,000+ years of strategic wisdom.

This is not just a cash flow strategy. It is a financial dharma—a path that honors both abundance and accountability.

Welcome to your new financial empire. Welcome to Provide Yourself First—the Chanakya way.

CHAPTER TWO

COMMON MISTAKE- 1: LACK OF BUDGETING

One of the most common mistakes entrepreneurs and businessmen make when managing cashflow is not budgeting properly. Without a budget, it can be challenging to keep track of your business's financial health, and you may end up overspending or underestimating expenses. This chapter will cover the most common budgeting mistakes and how to avoid them.

Section 1.1: Not setting clear financial goals

One of the most critical aspects of effective budgeting is setting clear financial goals. Without a clear set of objectives, it can be challenging to allocate funds in the right areas, which can lead to overspending on unnecessary expenses. It is essential to set specific financial goals for your business, such as increasing revenue or reducing expenses, and to create a budget that aligns with those goals.

To achieve these goals, it is essential to have a comprehensive understanding of your business's financial situation. This includes analyzing your revenue streams, identifying your expenses, and examining your cash flow.

Once you have a clear idea of your financial situation, you can begin to develop a budget that will help you achieve your goals. It is also crucial to revisit your financial goals regularly and adjust your budget accordingly to ensure that your business's finances stay on track. By setting clear financial goals and regularly reviewing your budget, you can ensure that your business is on a path to long-term financial success.

Section 1.2: Underestimating expenses

When it comes to budgeting for your business, it's crucial to be realistic and thorough. One common mistake that businesses make is underestimating expenses. This can lead to cashflow problems and hinder your ability to achieve your business goals. By underestimating expenses, you risk overspending and may not have enough funds to cover unexpected costs.

To avoid underestimating expenses, it's essential to track your expenses regularly. Keeping a detailed record of all your business expenses is an important step in identifying areas where you may be overspending or underestimating costs. By reviewing your expenses regularly, you can adjust your budget accordingly and make informed decisions regarding your finances. It's important to be flexible with your budget and make changes when necessary to ensure that you remain on track to achieve your business goals.

In addition, it's vital to factor in unexpected expenses when creating your budget. While it's impossible to predict every expense that may arise, having a contingency plan in place can help you avoid financial hardship. Consider setting aside a portion of your budget for unexpected expenses or establishing an emergency fund. This way, if unexpected costs arise, you can cover them without disrupting your overall budget. By being thorough and realistic in your budgeting process, you can

Section 1.3: Ignoring cash reserves

As a business owner, it is crucial to plan for the unexpected, and having a cash reserve in place is a critical component of that planning. A cash reserve acts as a safety net for your business, allowing you to cover unexpected expenses or weather short-term cashflow problems without impacting your day-to-day operations.

When creating your budget, it is important to factor in the need for a cash reserve. A good rule of thumb is to have at least three to six months of operating expenses saved in reserve. However, the amount you set aside will depend on the size of your business, its cashflow, and the level of risk you are willing to take on. It is also important to regularly review and adjust your cash reserve to ensure it is sufficient to cover your needs.

Having a cash reserve in place can give you peace of mind in uncertain times and allow you to focus on growing your business. It can also help you to maintain a good credit score by avoiding late payments or missed bills. By making a habit of setting aside money for a cash reserve, you can protect your business from potential financial hardships and ensure your continued success.

CHAPTER THREE

COMMON MISTAKE- 2: POOR RECORD-KEEPING

One of the most critical aspects of running a successful business is managing cashflow effectively. Unfortunately, many entrepreneurs and businessmen make common mistakes when it comes to cashflow management, and one of these is poor record-keeping. Without accurate financial records, it can be challenging to keep track of your business's cashflow and identify areas where you may be overspending. This can lead to serious financial consequences, including cash shortages, missed payments, and even bankruptcy.

To avoid poor record-keeping, it's essential to establish a system for tracking all financial transactions, including income, expenses, and investments. This system should be easy to use and understand, allowing you to quickly and accurately record all financial data. You may want to invest in accounting software or hire a professional accountant to help you set up and manage your financial records.

Additionally, it's important to regularly review and update your records, ensuring that they are up to date and accurate. By maintaining accurate financial records, you can gain a better understanding of your business's cashflow and make informed decisions that will help you achieve your financial goals.

Section 2.1: Disorganized financial records

Maintaining organized financial records is essential for the success of any business. Disorganized financial records can lead to serious consequences, such as inaccurate financial reports, missed deadlines for payments, and even legal issues. To avoid such situations, it is crucial to implement a system for organizing and maintaining financial records.

The first step in organizing financial records is to designate a specific location to store all financial documents. This can be a physical file cabinet, a dedicated folder on your computer or cloud-based storage, or a combination of both. Once you have a designated storage location, it is important to keep your records up to date and categorize them by type, date, and other relevant information. This will make it easier to find the information you need quickly and efficiently, allowing you to make informed financial decisions for your business. By prioritizing organization and accuracy in financial record-keeping, you can ensure the financial success and longevity of your business.

Section 2.2: Not tracking expenses and income regularly

One of the most common mistakes that business owners make when it comes to record-keeping is not tracking expenses and income regularly. This can lead to a variety of problems, including overspending, inaccurate forecasting of cash flow, and difficulty identifying areas where you may be able to save money. To avoid these issues, it is crucial to establish a system for tracking expenses and income regularly.

One effective method for keeping track of your business's expenses and income is to use a spreadsheet or accounting software. This allows you to easily log all transactions and keep a running tally of your income and expenses. Additionally, it is important to make sure that you update your records regularly, ideally on a daily or weekly basis, to ensure that you have accurate and up-to-date information at all times. By staying on top of your record-keeping, you can identify potential problems early and make adjustments to your budget or spending habits as needed, helping to ensure the long-term success of your business.

Section 2.3: Forgetting to log cash transactions

Finally, as a responsible and efficient financial manager, it is crucial to ensure that all cash transactions are meticulously logged and recorded. Every cash transaction, no matter how small, should be documented to avoid discrepancies in the budgeting process. It is essential to keep track of all cash transactions, including petty cash expenses and cash deposits, to maintain an accurate record of where the company's cash is going.

Failure to document cash transactions can lead to serious financial errors and mismanagement. It may also result in lost revenue opportunities, incorrect financial reporting, and difficulty identifying discrepancies in the company's accounting records. As such, it is vital to log all cash transactions in a timely and organized manner. Regularly reviewing and reconciling your cash records can help identify any gaps or inaccuracies, allowing for quick corrective action to be taken. Ultimately, keeping a detailed record of cash transactions is key to maintaining a healthy financial system and ensuring that the company is operating within its budget constraints.

CHAPTER FOUR

COMMON MISTAKE- 3: DELAYING INVOICING AND COLLECTIONS

Invoicing and collections are critical elements of managing cashflow. Delaying invoicing and collections can cashflow problems, missed payments, and other financial difficulties. This chapter will cover the most common invoicing and collections mistakes and how to avoid them.

Section 3.1: Waiting too long to send invoices

Invoicing is a critical component of running a successful business, and it's important to avoid common mistakes that can impact your cash flow and financial stability. One of the most significant invoicing mistakes is waiting too long to send invoices. This can result in delayed payments, making it challenging to track cash flow accurately and plan for the future. It can also create confusion for clients who may forget about the invoice or have questions about the amount owed.

To prevent this mistake, it's essential to develop a system for invoicing that works for your business. This may involve using invoicing software that automatically generates invoices and sends them to clients or setting up a schedule for manual invoicing. Additionally, it's important to follow up on any unpaid invoices promptly. This can involve sending reminders or making phone calls to clients who have not yet paid. By staying on top of invoicing and payment processes, you can ensure that your business operates smoothly and remains financially stable.

Section 3.2: Not following up on overdue payments

Invoicing is a critical aspect of any business, and even the slightest mistake could lead to serious financial consequences. One of the most common invoicing mistakes that many businesses make is failing to follow up on overdue payments. This oversight can have a significant impact on the company's cash flow, and if not addressed promptly, it could result in financial instability.

To avoid this mistake, businesses must have a robust invoicing system in place that includes regular follow-ups on overdue payments. This can be done by setting up automated reminders to customers who haven't paid or sending personalized emails or phone calls to clients who are behind on payments. It's also essential to be clear about payment terms and deadlines upfront and to communicate any changes in payment policies to customers promptly. Additionally, businesses can consider implementing late payment fees, which serve as an incentive for customers to pay on time and could help offset the cost of late payments.

In conclusion, following up on overdue payments is crucial for maintaining the financial health of a business.

By having a reliable invoicing system and implementing effective payment strategies, businesses can avoid the negative consequences of overdue payments, such as cash flow problems and financial instability. With proper invoicing techniques, businesses can ensure timely payments, maintain positive relationships with

Section 3.3: Not having a clear payment policy

One of the most crucial aspects of running a successful business is having a clear payment policy. As a business owner, you should be aware that without a clear payment policy in place, it can be incredibly challenging to enforce payment terms and collect payments owed to you. This can lead to a negative impact on your cash flow, causing significant financial stress and even jeopardizing the future of your business.

To avoid these potential issues, it is highly recommended that you create a clear payment policy that outlines all relevant payment terms and conditions. This should include details such as payment deadlines, accepted payment methods, late payment fees, and any other relevant information. It is also important to communicate your payment policy effectively to all customers, whether through email, phone, or in-person meetings. By including your payment policy in your contracts and invoices, you can ensure that your customers are aware of your terms and that you have a clear understanding of your payment expectations. Overall, establishing a clear payment policy is an essential step towards building a successful and sustainable business.

CHAPTER FIVE

COMMON MISTAKE- 4: OVERSPENDING AND OVERINVESTING

Managing cash flow is one of the most important tasks of any business owner. Overspending and overinvesting are two common mistakes that can cause cash flow problems and put your business at risk. Overspending refers to spending beyond what is necessary, while overinvesting refers to investing too much money in areas that may not provide a significant return on investment.

One common mistake of overspending is not having a budget or not sticking to it. It is important to create a budget and track expenses to ensure that spending is within the limits of the business's finances. Another mistake is spending on unnecessary or frivolous items, such as luxury office equipment or expensive company outings. Business owners should prioritize spending on items that are essential to the operations of the business and have a positive impact on revenue.

On the other hand, overinvesting can occur when business owners put too much money into non-essential areas, such as excessive marketing or hiring more employees than necessary. It is important to assess the return on investment for any investment made and determine if it is worth the cost. Business owners should also consider alternative investments that can provide a higher return on investment or that are more aligned with the goals and needs of the business. By avoiding these common mistakes, business owners

Section 4.1: Spending on unnecessary expenses

As a business owner, it is essential to understand the importance of managing expenses effectively to avoid overspending. One of the most significant mistakes that business owners make is spending on unnecessary expenses. These expenses do not contribute to the success of the business, and overspending on them can lead to cash flow problems and put the business at risk.

To avoid this, it is crucial to review expenses regularly and identify areas where you can cut back. Look for ways to negotiate better prices with vendors, switch to more cost-effective alternatives, and reduce non-essential expenses. You may also consider conducting a cost-benefit analysis of your business expenses to determine which ones are necessary for the success of your business and which ones are not. This will help you make informed decisions on where to allocate your resources and ensure that you are only spending on the expenses that are essential to the growth of your business. By effectively managing your expenses, you can improve your cash flow, reduce financial stress, and increase the profitability of your business.

Section 4.2: Not prioritizing investments

Many business owners make the mistake of not prioritizing investments, which can lead to wasted resources and missed opportunities. While investing in your business can be beneficial, it's important to be strategic about where those investments go. One of the keys to successful investment prioritization is identifying your business's most critical needs. This requires a thorough understanding of your business's current state, as well as its goals and aspirations.

Once you've identified your business's most critical needs, the next step is to prioritize investments that will address those needs. This involves considering the potential return on investment (ROI) of each investment opportunity, and focusing on those that will provide the most significant impact on your business's success. By taking a strategic approach to investment prioritization, you can ensure that your business is making the most of its resources and positioning itself for long-term growth and success.

Section 4.3: Taking on too much debt

In today's competitive business world, it is essential to have a clear understanding of debt and its impact on your business. While debt can be a useful tool for growing your business, it is important to be cautious and to thoroughly research your options before taking on any new debt. When considering debt, it is crucial to assess your business's ability to repay the debt and to determine the appropriate amount of debt to take on.

Moreover, it is crucial to have a clear debt repayment plan that aligns with your business's cash flow. A debt repayment plan outlines how the debt will be repaid over a certain period based on the business's revenue projections. With a repayment plan in place, you can ensure that you are on track to repay the debt and avoid any potential default that could damage your credit score and hinder future financing opportunities. Additionally, seeking alternative forms of financing, such as equity financing or crowdfunding, can provide a way to grow your business without taking on excessive debt. By carefully considering your options and creating a solid plan, you can use debt to your advantage and propel your business forward.

CHAPTER SIX

COMMON MISTAKE- 5: MISMANAGING CASHFLOW DURING GROWTH PHASES

Growth phases are critical periods in any business's journey, and entrepreneurs and businessmen must approach them with caution. While growth brings new opportunities, it also increases the risks involved. One of the most significant risks is mismanaging cashflow, which can cause a range of financial difficulties for a business. Therefore, it is essential to have a solid understanding of cashflow management and avoid the common mistakes that entrepreneurs make during growth phases.

One of the most common cashflow management mistakes during growth phases is failing to plan for the increased demand for working capital. As sales increase, so does the need for inventory, raw materials, and labor, all of which require cash. If a business does not plan for this increased demand, it may struggle to meet its obligations, leading to missed opportunities and strained relationships with suppliers and customers. Therefore, businesses must accurately forecast their cashflow requirements and secure sufficient financing to meet their needs. By planning ahead, businesses can avoid cashflow problems during growth phases and capitalize on new opportunities.

Section 5.1: Expanding too quickly

Among the most common mistakes made by businesses during growth phases is expanding too quickly. While growth is an essential component of any business, it is critical to grow at a sustainable pace that aligns with your financial goals. This is because, without proper cash flow management, businesses may find themselves struggling to stay afloat due to the costs associated with expansion.

To avoid this common pitfall, businesses must create a growth plan that aligns with their financial goals. This plan should take into account the financial impact of growth and ensure that the company has the necessary resources to support that growth. Moreover, businesses should consider alternative growth strategies, such as partnerships or joint ventures, that may help them grow without taking on excessive risk. These strategies can provide businesses with the resources and expertise they need to expand while avoiding the potential pitfalls of rapid expansion. Overall, it is essential that businesses prioritize financial planning and cash flow management during any growth phase to ensure long-term success.

Section 5.2: Not forecasting cashflow during growth

One of the most significant challenges faced by business owners is managing their finances effectively. While many entrepreneurs are passionate about their products or services, they may not have the financial acumen required to run a successful business. One common mistake that business owners make is failing to forecast cash flow during growth phases. As a business expands, it requires more resources, and managing finances becomes increasingly complex. Failing to forecast cash flow accurately can lead to cash flow problems, which can put a business at risk of insolvency.

To avoid this mistake, business owners must create a cash flow forecast that takes into account their growth plans. They need to consider the financial impact of their growth strategy and make sure they adjust their budget and cash reserves accordingly. A cash flow forecast will help business owners identify potential cash flow problems in advance, giving them time to take corrective action. Moreover, it will help them identify opportunities for growth and make informed decisions about investments. By forecasting cash flow accurately, businesses can plan their future growth with confidence and ensure their long-term success.

Section 5.3: Not having a contingency plan

When it comes to growing a business, having a contingency plan is a crucial step in ensuring its success. Every business has its ups and downs, and unexpected events can happen at any time. These events can cause a significant impact on your business's cash flow, which can make it difficult for you to manage your finances and stay afloat. Therefore, a contingency plan is essential to minimize risks and protect your business.

A well-thought-out contingency plan should consider all potential risks and outline how to deal with them. This includes outlining steps to take when faced with unexpected events, such as a sudden decrease in sales or an unforeseen expense. Your contingency plan should also include a budget for unexpected events and enough cash reserves to cover your expenses during difficult times. Having a contingency plan in place will give you peace of mind and ensure that your business can survive any unexpected event that comes your way.

CHAPTER SEVEN

Common Mistake- 6: Not Managing Cashflow Profitably

Managing the cash flow in a business is a crucial part of staying profitable, yet many entrepreneurs struggle to keep their finances in order. That's where the Profit First method comes in. Created by Mike Michalowicz, this system focuses on prioritizing profitability from the very start, rather than considering it an afterthought. Implementing this method in your business can greatly improve your financial health and overall success.

The principles of Profit First are simple. The first step is to take your revenue and allocate it to different expense categories, such as operating expenses, owner's compensation, taxes and profit. However, the unique aspect of this system is the order in which these categories are prioritized. Most businesses typically pay their expenses and then see what's leftover for profit. Instead, Profit First advocates allocating profit first, before expenses.

This may seem counterintuitive, but allocating profit as a priority forces a business to prioritize expense management and be more efficient with spending. When you have limited funds to work with, you become more creative and resourceful in finding ways to cut costs and increase revenue. It also creates a more financially stable business, as you have a cushion of savings to rely on if unexpected expenses arise.

Profit First also emphasizes the mentality of being more mindful of expenses. By allotting a specific amount of money to each expense category, you are forced to evaluate your expenses more carefully and assess where you can make adjustments. It's like implementing a personal budget for your business.

Many successful businesses have implemented the Profit First method with great results. One example is Precision Nutrition, a nutrition coaching company that experienced financial struggles in their early years. After implementing Profit First, they turned their financial situation around and became a more stable and profitable business. Another example is The Bean Ninjas, an accounting company that used to struggle with consistent profits. After adopting the Profit First method, they now have a stable cash flow and healthy profit margins.

If you're interested in implementing the Profit First method in your own business, there are several actionable steps you can take:

1. Determine your revenue and allocate it to specific categories: operating expenses, owner's compensation,

taxes, and profit.

2. Determine your target profit percentage and allocate that amount to your "profit" category.

3. Make adjustments to your expenses and find ways to reduce costs. For example, evaluate your subscriptions and see which ones you can eliminate or downgrade.

4. Re-evaluate and adjust your allocations on a quarterly basis to ensure you're on track with your targets.

One potential challenge with implementing the Profit First method is the fear of not having enough money for expenses. However, this method forces you to be more mindful and efficient with expenses, and it's unlikely that you'll run out of funds for necessary expenses. If you do find yourself with limited funds, it may be a sign that adjustments need to be made to your expenses.

Overall, the Profit First method can greatly improve the financial health of your business and create a more stable and efficient cash flow. By prioritizing profit and being more mindful of expenses, you'll be able to achieve long-term success and profitability.

Conclusion

In this eBook, we have discussed the most common mistakes entrepreneurs and businessmen make when managing cashflow and how to avoid them. By avoiding these mistakes and implementing best practices for cashflow management, you can ensure that your business remains financially healthy and successful.

Tips for successful cashflow management

Here are some tips for successful cashflow management:

- **Create a budget and stick to it**
- **Track your business's expenses and income regularly**

- Send invoices promptly and follow up on overdue payments
- Invest in your business wisely
- Plan for growth and have a contingency plan in place
- Learn to manage cashflow – profitably using 'Profit First' Method

Final thoughts and next steps

Managing cashflow profitable can be challenging, but it's essential for the success of your business. By avoiding common mistakes and implementing best practices for cashflow management, you can ensure that your business remains financially healthy and successful.

If you're struggling with cashflow management, consider seeking the advice of a financial professional or business coach. They can provide you with valuable insights and strategies your business's cashflow effectively.

Chanakya's Sutras' Importance and Applicationin Modern Business Cashflow Management

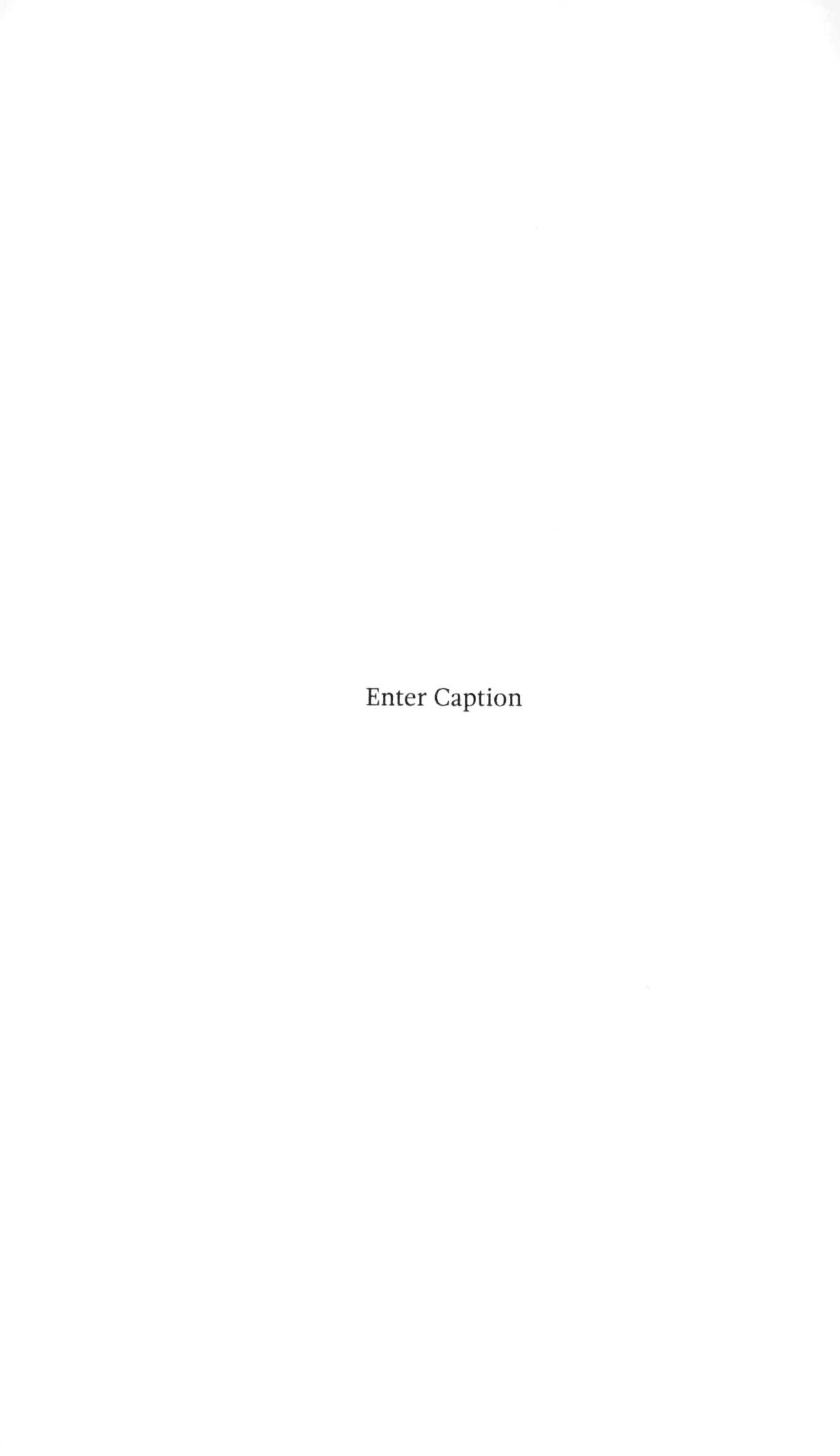

CHAPTER EIGHT

ARTHASYA MOOLAM RAKSHANAM – THE ROOT OF WEALTH IS PRESERVATION

Sutra Context

"Arthasya Moolam Rakshanam" – Chanakya's wisdom begins not with creation, but with preservation. Wealth, he says, must be protected even before it is accumulated further. This is counterintuitive in a world that constantly chases more – more revenue, more customers, more growth. Yet, without safeguarding what you earn, even the most successful business is financially vulnerable.

In ancient times, kings maintained well-guarded treasuries, ensuring that the state would survive through droughts, wars, or disasters. Chanakya advised rulers to first build strong reserves before embarking on ambitious public projects. For business owners today, the principle is the same: **if you don't protect your profits, you will remain trapped in the cycle of earning and spending, never truly becoming wealthy.**

Modern Application in Business Finance

Most entrepreneurs operate on a reactive financial model:

- They earn revenue,
- Cover expenses,
- Pay taxes,
- And *hope* there's some profit left over.

This backward approach is the reason why businesses struggle with cash flow despite strong top-line growth. The key lesson from Chanakya is this: **we must reverse the formula** – take profit first and design the business to run on what remains.

Profit Maximiser Principle: "Provide Yourself First"

The modern-day Profit Maximiser system, inspired by Mike Michalowicz's *Profit First* philosophy, aligns perfectly with Chanakya's sutra. It operationalizes wealth preservation through intentional cash allocation:

Revenue – Profit – Tax – Owner's Pay = Expenses

By pre-allocating profit every time revenue comes in, we ensure that wealth is preserved and not accidentally consumed. This structure builds a business model that rewards the entrepreneur, maintains stability, and forces efficient operations.

How to Integrate This into Your Business

Step 1: Open Multiple Bank Accounts

Create dedicated accounts for the following purposes:

1. **Income Account** – All business revenues land here first.
2. **Profit Account** – Allocate a fixed % (start with 5%) from each income deposit.
3. **Tax Account** – Allocate 10–15% for tax obligations.
4. **Owner's Pay Account** – Pay yourself a fixed amount (based on a % of revenue).
5. **Operating Expenses (OPEX) Account** – What's left is used for running the business.

This separation is the modern treasury system – just like a king would divide resources between war, welfare, and reserves.

Step 2: Set Your Allocation Percentages (TAP – Target Allocation Percentages)

Revenue Band	Profit	Tax	Owner's Pay	OPEX
₹0–10L	5%	10%	50%	35%
₹10L–50L	10%	15%	35%	40%
₹50L+	15%	15%	30%	40%

Note: Adjust these percentages based on your business maturity and financial goals.

Step 3: Conduct a Cash Flow Diagnostic

- Review your last 6 months of revenue and expenses.
- Calculate what % you could have saved as profit.
- Identify leaks in spending (subscriptions, unproductive salaries, impulse investments).

Step 4: Implement the Profit Transfer Rhythm

- **Every 10th and 25th of the month**, transfer allocations based on the revenue received.
- Treat profit like a **non-negotiable cost of doing business**, just like rent or salaries.

Business Case Study – Meet Anjali, a Boutique Owner
Anjali runs a profitable clothing brand in Pune. Despite ₹80L in annual revenue, she had almost zero savings at year-end. After implementing the "Provide Yourself First" system:

- She began allocating 8% to her profit account.
- Paid herself ₹60,000 monthly as Owner's Pay (instead of random withdrawals).
- Cut 20% of her operating costs by questioning every rupee spent.

Within 6 months, she had ₹3.2L in her Profit account – her first real savings in 3 years of business.
End-of-Chapter Action Steps

- Open 5 separate business bank accounts.
- Decide your starting allocation percentages.
- Review your past 6 months' cash flow.
- Set a bi-monthly Profit Allocation Schedule.

- Transfer your first profit share – even if it's ₹500.
- Make profit preservation a ritual, not a reward.

Final Reflection

Preservation is not about hoarding wealth; it's about ensuring your business serves *you*, not just your clients or staff. Profit is not an afterthought – it is the **reason** your business exists.

By implementing this first sutra – *Arthasya Moolam Rakshanam* – through the Profit Maximiser system, you set the foundation for a secure, sustainable, and scalable business.

Next: We move to Chanakya's principle on financial effort – *"Arthasya Moolam Udyamah"* – and how consistent, focused enterprise feeds the profit engine you've just protected.

CHAPTER NINE

ARTHASYA MOOLAM UDYAMAH – THE ROOT OF WEALTH IS ENTERPRISE

Sutra Context

"Arthasya Moolam Udyamah" – According to Chanakya, wealth is not created by chance, inheritance, or luck. It is created through Udyamah – focused effort, industriousness, and enterprise. This principle highlights a profound truth: only through active pursuit, persistence, and purposeful work does wealth become a reality.

Chanakya observed that kingdoms, like individuals, must strive and act to achieve prosperity. For entrepreneurs, this means developing systems, discipline, and habits that convert energy and ideas into results – consistently and repeatedly.

Modern Application in Business Finance

Most businesses today start with a burst of enthusiasm but often lose steam when challenges arise. While external capital or occasional sales spikes can offer temporary boosts, they are not substitutes for consistent action and disciplined operations.

Chanakya's teaching of Udyamah reminds us that there is no shortcut to sustainable wealth. It must be earned through repeated and intelligent enterprise.

Sporadic effort creates unpredictable results. Strategic effort compounds wealth.

Profit Maximiser Principle: Build a Consistent Revenue Engine

The Profit Maximiser system thrives on predictable income. Taking profit first only works when there is a steady stream of inflows to allocate from. Therefore, consistent marketing, sales efforts, and client delivery become non-negotiable.

The modern interpretation of *Udyamah* is:

- Build systems that attract leads.
- Convert leads into sales with discipline.
- Deliver services efficiently.
- Repeat. Refine. Repeat.

In the absence of this operational rhythm, cash flow dries up, and the business becomes reactive instead of proactive.

How to Integrate "Enterprise" into Your Profit Maximiser System

Step 1: Create a Weekly Revenue Routine

- Block dedicated time every week for sales-generating activities.
- Examples: client follow-ups, webinars, LinkedIn outreach, email marketing.
- Use a KPI dashboard to track lead-to-sale conversion.

Step 2: Install a Simple Sales System

- Create a sales pipeline to manage leads from inquiry to payment.
- Use CRM tools or even a spreadsheet to track each prospect.
- Automate follow-ups using email or WhatsApp to reduce manual chasing.

Step 3: Package Your Services for Scalability

- Move from custom quotes to predefined packages.
- Productize your offerings with clear pricing and outcomes.
- This speeds up sales and ensures consistent revenue patterns.

Step 4: Commit to a Marketing Cadence

- Choose 1–2 marketing channels (e.g., Instagram + Email).
- Post valuable content regularly to attract leads.
- Use scheduling tools to stay consistent.

Step 5: Align Team or Freelancer Tasks to Revenue Goals

- Link weekly deliverables to income-focused outcomes.
- Example: A content writer writes 2 lead-generation blog posts/week.
- Avoid overstaffing until profit allocations are consistent.

Business Case Study – Rajeev, a Chartered Accountant Rajeev ran a CA practice for 5 years, but growth plateaued. After implementing the *Udyamah* principle:

- He blocked 3 hours every Monday for sales calls and email follow-ups.
- Created fixed-fee packages for tax planning, audits, and monthly compliance.
- Delegated non-core tasks and focused only on high-value activities.

His revenue increased by 37% in 6 months, and he made his first quarterly profit allocation.
End-of-Chapter Action Steps

- Block 3–5 hours weekly for sales and income-producing tasks.
- Create a lead-tracking sheet or simple CRM to track conversions.
- Define 2–3 service packages with fixed pricing.
- Publish content consistently to generate leads.
- Align team roles with revenue objectives.
- Review weekly revenue performance using a simple scorecard.

Final Reflection

Effort is not a one-time push – it is a rhythm. Chanakya's *Udyamah* teaches us that building wealth is about showing up repeatedly with purpose and precision. Profit does not come from occasional inspiration but from structured enterprise.

With your Profit Maximiser system in place, *Udyamah* ensures the inflow continues. It transforms your business from a hope-based operation to a profit-predictable engine.

In the next chapter, we explore *"Arthasya Moolam Seva"* – the idea that service, not selling, is the deepest source of wealth and trust in business.

CHAPTER TEN

ARTHASYA MOOLAM SEVA – THE ROOT OF WEALTH IS SERVICE

Sutra Context

"Arthasya Moolam Seva" – Chanakya declared that wealth is not generated by manipulation or exploitation, but by **genuine service**. This teaching shifts the focus of entrepreneurship from "what can I sell?" to "how can I serve?". When businesses solve real problems, meet real needs, and add real value, wealth flows as a byproduct.

In ancient kingdoms, trade and commerce thrived in places where merchants were known for fairness, quality, and service. Chanakya understood that the prosperity of a nation or business is rooted in the **trust and utility it creates for others**.

Modern Application in Business Finance

In today's transactional world, service is often treated as a department – not a mindset. Businesses chase revenue by pushing products rather than understanding and solving problems. This leads to churn, inconsistent cash flow, and poor word-of-mouth.

Chanakya reminds us: when **service is embedded in your business model**, profit becomes inevitable. Customers return, refer others, and pay you gladly. Your revenue becomes more consistent, your expenses reduce (less marketing, less refunds), and your cash flow improves.

Service builds trust. Trust builds loyalty. Loyalty builds profit.

Profit Maximiser Principle: Serve First, Profit Always

The Profit Maximiser system becomes more powerful when it is *value-led*. When your offerings genuinely help your customer:

- Refunds reduce.
- Referrals increase.
- You can command premium pricing.

Instead of chasing more leads or deeper funnels, ask:

- "Is my offer solving a burning problem?"
- "Is my onboarding smooth?"
- "Is my support consistent and caring?"

These questions don't just improve service; they drive financial outcomes.

How to Integrate "Seva" into Your Profit Maximiser System

Step 1: Redesign Your Offer Around a Transformation

- Don't sell services. Sell outcomes.
- Define the **before and after** state for every offer.
- Example: A tax consultant isn't selling returns. He's selling **peace of mind and penalty avoidance**.

Step 2: Build a Customer Experience Map

- Document the **touchpoints** your customer experiences – from lead to delivery.
- Improve at least one step per month (onboarding emails, delivery templates, support speed).

Step 3: Add Feedback Loops into Cashflow Planning

- After every 5th or 10th client, collect structured feedback.
- Use feedback to improve offer design or remove operational inefficiencies.
- Delighted clients pay faster, refer more, and stay longer.

Step 4: Define and Deliver a "Service Bonus"

- Offer an unexpected free upgrade or bonus in your delivery.
- Example: A digital marketer includes a bonus audit report.
- The goal is to exceed expectations without hurting margins.

Step 5: Create Service-Driven Marketing

- Share client wins, testimonials, and case studies.
- Let your *service record* be your best sales copy.
- Serve through content: educate, simplify, and support.

Business Case Study – Aditi, Personal Branding Coach

Aditi was struggling to scale her coaching program. Her cash flow was erratic, and she had a high churn rate. After applying the Seva mindset:

- She simplified her onboarding and added a personal video welcome.
- Introduced a **90-day transformation roadmap** with milestones.
- Added a monthly 15-minute check-in call for every active client.

Results: Her renewal rate jumped by 50%, client referrals tripled, and she built a 3-month emergency fund from profit allocations alone.

End-of-Chapter Action Steps

- Redesign your offer to focus on client transformation.
- Map and improve your customer experience journey.
- Schedule regular feedback and apply learnings.
- Surprise your clients with a service bonus.
- Build content that teaches, helps, or inspires.
- Review how service improvements reflect in your cash flow.

Final Reflection

Seva is not soft. It is smart. A business built on service does not chase money – money follows it. When your clients feel seen, helped, and valued, they stay. They pay. They tell others.

Chanakya's sutra *"Arthasya Moolam Seva"* reminds us: **service is the most profitable investment**. Integrated with the Profit Maximiser method, it ensures your business is not just profitable, but respected, recommended, and resilient.

In the next chapter, we'll explore *"Na asti avyayam dhanam"* – how disciplined spending turns retained earnings into real wealth.

CHAPTER ELEVEN

Na asti avyayam dhanam – There is No Wealth Without Financial Prudence

Sutra Context

"Na asti avyayam dhanam" – In Chanakya's worldview, true wealth is not just about earning more, but **spending wisely**. He warned that even the largest of treasuries would deplete without discipline. Unchecked spending leads to scarcity, no matter how great the income.

Chanakya's advice to kings was clear: treat public wealth with care, avoid impulsive expenses, and demand accountability. The same rule applies to modern business owners. A profitable top line means little if your bottom line leaks due to waste, indulgence, or inefficiency.

Earning is a skill. Preserving is a discipline.

Modern Application in Business Finance

In the digital economy, it's easier than ever to spend money mindlessly:

- One-click SaaS subscriptions.
- Ads that drain budgets without ROI.
- Hiring before profits stabilize.

A business that earns ₹10L but spends ₹9.5L isn't wealthy—it's just surviving. Financial prudence ensures that profit isn't theoretical—it is banked, used purposefully, and multiplied.

Chanakya teaches that **frugality is not about being cheap**—it's about being conscious. Spend like a king who rules wisely, not like one who entertains his court for applause.

Profit Maximiser Principle: Force Frugality Through Allocation

The genius of the Profit Maximiser system is that it enforces discipline. By allocating your income first into **Profit, Tax,** and **Owner's Pay**, you limit what is left for Operating Expenses (OPEX). This forces your business to operate within **conscious constraints**.

You no longer spend and hope for profit. You spend only what is available *after* securing your profit.

How to Integrate Financial Prudence into Profit Maximiser

Step 1: Cap Your OPEX – Create "Reverse Budgets"

- After allocating for Profit, Tax, and Pay, the remaining amount is your **OPEX ceiling**.
- Operate strictly within this amount.
- If you can't afford something today, **you don't buy it today.**

Step 2: Audit Recurring Expenses Every Quarter

- Review subscriptions, staff overheads, tools, and platforms.
- Cancel underused or unproductive tools.
- Negotiate rates with vendors or move to leaner alternatives.

Step 3: Separate Needs from Wants

- Before any spend, ask: "Is this expense driving revenue or stability?"
- Delay wants for 30 days; most impulses vanish.
- Implement a team-wide "₹0-based budget mindset."

Step 4: Use an OPEX Scorecard

- Track monthly spend in categories: People, Tools, Rent, Marketing.
- Create a score (1–5) for ROI per category.
- Identify which costs deliver returns—and which are vanity.

Step 5: Build a "Do More With Less" Culture

- Celebrate frugality in team meetings.
- Reward employees who optimize costs.

- Replace the idea of "big budgets = growth" with "smart spending = agility."

Business Case Study – Nikhil, Tech Agency Owner

Nikhil ran a growing web development firm but always struggled with month-end stress. His revenue was ₹ 1.5Cr annually, but his expenses ballooned with new hires, marketing tools, and fancy office upgrades.

After applying Chanakya's principle:

- He shifted to a 40% OPEX cap using the Profit Maximiser model.
- Cancelled 9 SaaS tools and renegotiated 3 vendor contracts.
- Delayed hiring and outsourced 2 functions instead.

Result: ₹12L in pure profit saved within 9 months—and his team productivity improved!

End-of-Chapter Action Steps

- Calculate your current OPEX as a % of revenue.
- Set a target OPEX ceiling (ideally 40–50%).
- Review and eliminate non-essential subscriptions/tools.
- Start a monthly expense review ritual.
- Reward cost-saving initiatives across your team.
- Only upgrade expenses when profit targets are consistently met.

Final Reflection

Spending is easy. But saving is an intentional act of leadership. Chanakya's lesson is clear: if you don't respect your money, no one else will—clients, team, or the market.

Financial prudence is how businesses build *real* wealth. It's not about denial—it's about direction. Every rupee saved is a rupee that can be reinvested, reserved, or returned to the entrepreneur.

As you continue applying the Profit Maximiser system, remember: **restraint is a superpower.** Next, we explore *"Rinam kritva na bhoktam"*—why debt-driven indulgence can destroy financial momentum.

CHAPTER TWELVE

RINAM KRITVA NA BHOKTAM – AVOID DEBT-FUELED INDULGENCE

Sutra Context

"Rinam Kritva Na Bhoktam" – Chanakya, ever the practical economist, warned: do not borrow just to indulge. In ancient times, kings who borrowed heavily to fund luxurious lifestyles lost their kingdoms. Debt, when not used wisely, enslaves the borrower and destroys future potential.

In modern business, this sutra is a wake-up call: **using loans or credit to fund expenses that don't generate income is a fast path to financial instability.** Whether it's borrowing to upgrade office space, splurging on unnecessary software, or extending payment terms to make ends meet—debt without discipline is dangerous.

Modern Application in Business Finance

Not all debt is bad. Strategic borrowing to fund revenue-generating activities—like inventory, marketing with clear ROI, or growth-focused capital expenditure—can help accelerate momentum. But borrowing to fund lifestyle upgrades, vanity projects, or to plug avoidable cash flow gaps? That's financial malpractice.

Debt is not evil. Indulgent debt is.

Chanakya's philosophy urges us to ask: Is this debt productive or parasitic?

Profit Maximiser Principle: Run on Real Revenue, Not Borrowed Fuel

The Profit Maximiser system works best when your business is running on actual income, not inflated cash from loans. By allocating revenue into **Profit, Tax, Owner's Pay**, and **OPEX**, you begin to operate within your means.

This creates financial boundaries that **remove the need for unnecessary borrowing**. If OPEX is insufficient, you adjust—not borrow. If growth requires investment, you save or bootstrap before seeking outside capital.

How to Integrate Debt Discipline into the Profit Maximiser System

Step 1: Categorize All Business Debt

- Divide existing debts into:

  - **Productive Debt**: drives income (e.g. marketing with clear ROI)
  - **Survival Debt**: used to plug short-term cash flow gaps
  - **Indulgent Debt**: used for status, aesthetics, or comfort

- Pay off indulgent debt first. Restructure or reduce survival debt.

Step 2: Ban Borrowing for Non-Essentials

- Create a **borrowing rulebook** for your business:

  - Borrow only when ROI can be reasonably projected.
  - Use debt only if repayment is feasible within 6–12 months.

- Ask: "Would I still spend on this if I had to use my profit, not debt?"

Step 3: Build a Debt Repayment Bucket in Your Allocation System

- Dedicate a percentage (5–10%) from each revenue cycle for debt reduction.
- Treat debt repayments like a **non-optional fixed cost**, not an afterthought.
- Consider this your "debt snowball" account.

Step 4: Create a Cash Reserve for Emergencies

- Build an **Emergency Buffer Fund** equal to 3–6 months of OPEX.
- Use this instead of credit cards, overdrafts, or emergency loans.
- Refill this fund every time it's used.

Step 5: Track Debt-to-Revenue Ratio Monthly

- Maintain a healthy **Debt-to-Revenue ratio** (ideally under 25%).
- If this crosses 30–35%, pause spending and focus on repayment.
- Make debt visibility a dashboard metric—not a hidden liability.

Business Case Study – Tanvi, a Digital Agency Owner
Tanvi scaled her team quickly using working capital loans and credit cards. Within 18 months:

- Her business made ₹90L in revenue.
- But she was paying ₹1.5L/month in EMIs.
- 80% of debt was for team, branding, and tools—not revenue growth.

After implementing this principle:

- She froze hiring, paused EMI-heavy expenses.
- Created a debt repayment account at 10% of revenue.
- Cleared 60% of debt within 9 months.

Her profit jumped from   ₹80K/month to   ₹2.2L/ month.
End-of-Chapter Action Steps

- Categorize current business debt into productive, survival, and indulgent.
- Create borrowing rules: only borrow if ROI is measurable and payback is clear.
- Allocate 5–10% of income to a debt repayment bucket.
- Build a 3–6 month emergency fund to avoid future borrowing.

- Track Debt-to-Revenue ratio monthly.
- Pause new non-essential expenses until current debt drops below 25% of revenue.

Final Reflection

Debt is not a sin. But **borrowing for indulgence is a symptom of weak leadership.** Chanakya urges us to live within our means—and grow from strength, not from splurges.

If you must borrow, let it be for transformation, not decoration. Let it be to multiply wealth, not patch pride.

The Profit Maximiser system, when implemented with Chanakya's *Rinam Kritva Na Bhoktam* principle, becomes not just a financial tool—but a discipline that keeps wealth in your control.

In the next chapter, we explore *"Arthasya Moolam Vipulah Sanchayah"* – why consistent accumulation of small surpluses creates unshakable business foundations.

CHAPTER THIRTEEN

ARTHASYA MOOLAM VIPULAH SANCHAYAH – WEALTH GROWS THROUGH CONSISTENT ACCUMULATION

Sutra Context

"Arthasya Moolam Vipulah Sanchayah" – Chanakya taught that wealth is not acquired through a single windfall but through **continuous and disciplined accumulation**. Just as a reservoir is filled drop by drop, financial security

is built through regular saving, profit-taking, and reinvestment.

This sutra is a timeless reminder: **big fortunes begin with small surpluses**. Wealth that grows steadily is far more resilient than wealth that arrives suddenly and is lost due to mismanagement.

Modern Application in Business Finance

Entrepreneurs often chase the "big deal," "viral launch," or "breakout month" to solve their money issues. But consistent cashflow and profit accumulation are the true indicators of financial health.

Chanakya's guidance emphasizes:

- Save consistently, even if the amount is small.
- Let your profit be automatic, not aspirational.
- Focus on **accumulation, not just acquisition**.

This mindset leads to compound results over time – and separates businesses that **survive** from those that **thrive**.

Consistency builds momentum. Momentum builds wealth.

Profit Maximiser Principle: Accumulate Profit First, Not Last

In the Profit Maximiser model, every revenue deposit triggers a **small but mandatory allocation to profit**. This ensures:

- You are always accumulating wealth.
- Profit becomes a habit, not an event.
- Even in slow months, your business remains financially intentional.

Chanakya's idea of *vipulah sanchayah* maps perfectly to this practice. Small, consistent transfers build up a reserve that becomes your **financial runway, reinvestment fund, or peace-of-mind account**.

How to Integrate the Accumulation Principle

Step 1: Automate Profit Transfers

- Every 10th and 25th of the month, transfer a fixed % of revenue to the Profit Account.
- Even if revenue is low, transfer *something*. The habit matters more than the amount.

Step 2: Start with 1% Profit if You Feel Stretched

- If your business is running tight, begin with just 1%.
- Increase gradually as you eliminate waste and improve pricing.
- Let accumulation adapt to your financial capacity.

Step 3: Celebrate Milestones Publicly (Internally)

- When your Profit Account hits ₹50K, ₹1L, or ₹5L – acknowledge it.
- This creates a culture of financial celebration and discipline.
- Team members will start thinking in "savings-first" terms too.

Step 4: Set Surplus Goals, Not Just Revenue Goals

- Don't just aim for ₹1Cr in annual revenue.
- Aim for ₹15L in accumulated, retained profit.
- Set quarterly and annual "accumulation KPIs."

Step 5: Reinvest With Intention, Not Emotion

- When your profit reserve grows, don't rush to spend it.
- Reinvest only if it will multiply returns – marketing with ROI, asset purchase, or training.
- Otherwise, keep accumulating until opportunities justify release.

Business Case Study – Harsh, Ecommerce Retailer
Harsh ran a home décor brand on Shopify. Revenue was good, but profits never stayed. After implementing consistent accumulation:

- Started with 2% profit allocation, increased to 10% in 9 months.
- Automated bi-monthly transfers to a hidden account.
- Delayed impulsive marketing spends and prioritized organic channels.

Result: Built ₹9L **in accumulated profit within 12 months.** Used ₹3L to launch a second product line – cash-funded.

End-of-Chapter Action Steps

- Set up an automated profit transfer every 10th and 25th.
- Begin with 1% profit allocation if needed – just get started.
- Track your cumulative profit monthly.
- Set profit milestones and celebrate them internally.
- Avoid using the profit account for operating shortfalls.
- Create a quarterly plan for surplus reinvestment or retention.

Final Reflection

Wealth is not what you earn—it's what you **keep consistently**. Chanakya's advice transcends time: fortune is created by **the one who saves relentlessly, not the one who earns extravagantly.**

With the Profit Maximiser system in place, the principle of *Vipulah Sanchayah* ensures you build unshakable reserves—step by step, profit by profit.

In the next chapter, we explore *"Sampadam Na Tyajet"* – the principle of never abandoning wealth once created, and how to protect your growing surplus.

CHAPTER FOURTEEN

Sampadam Na Tyajet – Never Abandon Accumulated Wealth

Sutra Context

"Sampadam Na Tyajet" – Chanakya's guidance was clear: once wealth is accumulated, **do not let it go wastefully or casually**. True financial wisdom lies not only in earning and saving but in **protecting** what has been built. Letting wealth slip away through careless management, emotional spending, or impulsive risk-taking reverses years of effort.

To a king, abandoning wealth meant weakened defences, eroded influence, and lost dignity. To a business owner, it means no reserves, no buffer, and a business always on the edge.

Building wealth is hard. Losing it is easy. Holding it requires wisdom.

Modern Application in Business Finance

Entrepreneurs often sabotage their financial progress after initial success:

- Profit accounts get raided for new cars or gadgets.
- Surplus funds get dumped into untested ventures.
- Emergency buffers are used for last-minute team bonuses or impulsive hires.

Chanakya urges us to treat accumulated wealth with reverence. Profit, once captured, must be **preserved, managed, and only strategically deployed.**

Profit Maximiser Principle: Protect the Profit Vault

In the Profit Maximiser system, your Profit Account is sacred. It's not an extra OPEX fund. It's a **reward, reserve, and reinvestment engine**. If you breach this intentionally, you weaken your system.

Chanakya's *Sampadam Na Tyajet* aligns perfectly with:

- Preserving profit for quarterly distributions.
- Using it for strategic upgrades only after deep review.
- Protecting it during low-revenue months instead of consuming it.

How to Preserve Accumulated Wealth in the Profit Maximiser System

Step 1: Use a Hidden or Difficult-to-Access Profit Account

- Move the Profit Account to a **separate bank or institution.**
- Do not link it to your business operating apps or dashboards.

- Make withdrawals possible only through manual authorisation.

Step 2: Establish Profit Withdrawal Rules

- Withdraw profit quarterly (not monthly).
- Use a 50:50 rule:

  ◦ 50% for owner reward (vacation, investment, bonus).
  ◦ 50% retained for growth fund (future-proofing, scaling).

- Delay access during lean or uncertain quarters.

Step 3: Apply a 7-Day Cooling Rule on Major Profit Spends

- When tempted to use profit for a "big opportunity," pause.
- Wait 7 days. Re-evaluate with your coach, CFO, or advisor.
- Spend only if it aligns with your 12-month strategic goals.

Step 4: Convert Some Profit to Long-Term Personal Assets

- Every year, transfer a portion of your profit into **non-business investments**:

  ◦ Mutual funds
  ◦ Real estate

- ◦ Fixed deposits

- This diversifies your wealth and keeps business and personal finances separate.

Step 5: Review Profit Usage History Every 6 Months

- Create a tracker of how past profits were used.
- Ask: did they yield ROI? Stability? Peace of mind?
- Adjust policies if too much profit is being consumed, not retained.

Business Case Study – Suresh, SaaS Founder
Suresh had a profitable SaaS business and built a profit vault of   ₹15L within 18 months. But then:

- He dipped into the account to fund a side-project without validation.
- Burned ₹7L and ended up with stalled growth in both ventures.

Post that experience:

- He moved profit to a liquid fund outside business reach.
- Enforced a quarterly distribution plan and used 50% to build personal assets.

Now, his profit vault is at   ₹22L and untouched for over 10 months.
End-of-Chapter Action Steps

- Move your profit account to a separate or hidden bank.

- Define clear quarterly rules for accessing and distributing profit.
- Use a 7-day delay rule before spending large portions of profit.
- Start converting annual profits into personal investments.
- Review your profit usage history every 6 months.
- Protect the profit vault like your business depends on it—because it does.

Final Reflection

Wealth that is not protected will quietly vanish. Chanakya's *Sampadam Na Tyajet* warns us: don't become casual just because you've succeeded once. Stay alert. Stay respectful. Stay disciplined.

The Profit Maximiser system gives you the tools. This sutra gives you the mindset. Together, they ensure your profit is not just generated—but preserved, grown, and celebrated.

In the next chapter, we explore "*Yogakshemam Vahamyaham*" – the ancient idea of ensuring your own well-being first, and how it aligns perfectly with the philosophy of "Provide Yourself First."

CHAPTER FIFTEEN

YOGAKSHEMAM VAHAMYAHAM – ENSURE YOUR OWN WELL-BEING FIRST

Sutra Context

"Yogakshemam Vahamyaham" – While this sutra is from the Bhagavad Gita, it resonates deeply with Chanakya's teachings on self-preservation and priority. It roughly translates to: *"I carry the responsibility for the well-being and security of those who act with purpose and faith."* Applied to business, it emphasizes the foundational concept of **providing for oneself first** before serving others.

Chanakya advised kings and administrators to secure their own resources, safety, and clarity before managing the needs of the state or allies. In modern entrepreneurship, this means ensuring your own financial wellness before overcommitting to employees, customers, vendors, or even expansion plans.

Modern Application in Business Finance

Too many business owners operate with a **martyr mindset:**

- Paying everyone else first (staff, rent, vendors), and leaving nothing for themselves.
- Reinvesting 100% of income back into the business while neglecting personal savings.
- Living off scraps in the hope that "someday" the business will pay back.

This leads to burnout, resentment, and ironically, **business failure due to poor personal stability**. Chanakya would call this a strategic mistake.

A financially insecure entrepreneur cannot lead a financially stable business.

Profit Maximiser Principle: Provide Yourself First

The central tenet of the Profit Maximiser system is this: **your business must exist to serve you, not the other way around.**

By allocating income to **Owner's Pay** as a fixed, protected percentage, you ensure:

- You get paid consistently.
- You build personal wealth alongside business growth.
- You stay motivated and make strategic decisions from a place of strength—not desperation.

This is not selfish. It's structurally sound leadership.

How to Apply 'Provide Yourself First' in the Profit Maximiser System

Step 1: Allocate Owner's Pay as a Priority Account

- Create a separate **Owner's Pay Account.**
- Allocate a fixed % of revenue (start with 20–35% based on business size).
- Pay yourself from this account every 10th and 25th.

Step 2: Define a Personal Minimum Viable Salary (MVS)

- Calculate the minimum amount needed monthly for your personal obligations.
- Ensure Owner's Pay covers this before any business upgrades or expansions.
- Scale this pay up gradually as profit improves.

Step 3: Protect Owner's Pay From Business Temptations

- Never use Owner's Pay funds to cover business shortfalls.
- If needed, reduce expenses—not your personal stability.
- This forces you to optimize OPEX and pricing.

Step 4: Track Annual Owner Compensation Growth

- Every quarter, review how much you've paid yourself.
- Aim to increase personal income by 10–20% annually.
- Celebrate progress and adjust allocations if business capacity increases.

Step 5: Build a Personal Emergency Buffer

- Move part of your Owner's Pay into a **personal reserve account.**

- Build at least 6 months' worth of personal expenses.
- This buffer gives you decision-making freedom and emotional security.

Business Case Study – Isha, Financial Consultant

Isha worked 60-hour weeks running a boutique finance firm but only paid herself irregularly. Her staff were paid on time, clients were happy—but she was stuck.

After implementing the 'Provide Yourself First' approach:

- Allocated 25% of monthly income to Owner's Pay.
- Paid herself ₹1.2L/month consistently.
- Created a 6-month personal buffer from her Owner's Pay over time.

Outcome: She made better hiring decisions, stopped underpricing, and scaled revenue by 30% in one year.
End-of-Chapter Action Steps

- Open a separate Owner's Pay Account.
- Set your Minimum Viable Salary and start with 20–35% allocation.
- Automate payments to yourself every 10th and 25th.
- Avoid using Owner's Pay for business shortfalls.
- Review and increase your compensation quarterly.
- Build a personal 6-month reserve using surplus Owner's Pay.

Final Reflection

Chanakya believed that a weak ruler could not protect a strong kingdom. A depleted entrepreneur cannot grow a profitable business.

By prioritizing your own financial well-being, you lead from power, not pressure. **The Profit Maximiser system honors this sutra by structurally embedding self-care into your business model.**

In the next chapter, we explore *"Arthasya Moolam Guptam Raksha"* – the principle of protecting wealth through discretion, and how to shield your profit system from leaks, theft, and misuse.

CHAPTER SIXTEEN

ARTHASYA MOOLAM GUPTAM RAKSHA – PROTECT WEALTH THROUGH DISCRETION

Chapter 9: Arthasya Moolam Guptam Raksha – Protect Wealth Through Discretion

Sutra Context

"Arthasya Moolam Guptam Raksha" – Chanakya believed that the **protection of wealth through discretion and secrecy** was essential to sustained prosperity. A king who flaunted his treasures invited war; a businessman who publicly revealed his financial reserves exposed himself to

risk.

Wealth is not only eroded through spending but also through exposure. Competitors, fraudsters, or even your own team may take advantage when financial data is openly or carelessly handled. Chanakya teaches that **discretion is a form of defense.**

Keep your vault full, your vision clear, and your mouth shut.

Modern Application in Business Finance

In today's world of oversharing and constant performance metrics, entrepreneurs feel pressure to showcase revenue, profit milestones, or fundraises. But public financial displays come at a cost:

- Envy and internal conflict within the team.
- Pressure to maintain appearances.
- External threats: theft, embezzlement, data breaches.

The wisest entrepreneurs operate **quietly, confidently, and securely.**

Profit Maximiser Principle: Make Profit Invisible and Untouchable

The Profit Maximiser system is built on separating profit from operational accounts. This supports the Chanakyan wisdom of guptam raksha – protecting the wealth **out of reach and out of sight.**

Profit is not for display. It's for preservation, future-proofing, and financial independence.

How to Secure Profit with Strategic Discretion

Step 1: Use a Hidden Profit Account

- Open your Profit Account at a **different bank.**

- Don't link it to your main banking dashboard or accounting tool.
- Ensure no automatic access or debit card is attached.

Step 2: Create Internal Confidentiality Norms

- Only essential personnel (owner/CFO) should access profit data.
- Avoid sharing real-time profit metrics with operational teams.
- Maintain confidentiality on Owner's Pay, bonuses, and reserves.

Step 3: Avoid Public Revenue or Profit Disclosures

- Resist the urge to showcase income screenshots or '₹1Cr month' milestones.
- Use customer impact stories, not income claims, in marketing.
- Keep your financial truth guarded—let results speak quietly.

Step 4: Invest Privately, Not for Public Applause

- When deploying profits (real estate, gold, mutual funds), do it silently.
- Avoid large lifestyle upgrades just after profit withdrawals.
- Let your wealth accumulate in peace.

Step 5: Conduct Periodic Financial Risk Audits

- Check for internal risks: employee access, software permissions, financial leakage.
- Review cyber protection on your banking and accounting systems.
- Ensure 2FA and alerts are in place for all money movements.

Business Case Study – Vikram, a Manufacturing Entrepreneur

Vikram's business saw rapid growth and hit ₹2Cr in annual revenue. Excited, he:

- Shared his revenue screenshots on LinkedIn.
- Upgraded to a larger office, bought a luxury car.
- Gave team-wide hikes based on perceived reserves.

6 months later:

- A key staff member poached half the client list.
- A cyber breach hit his connected banking system.
- He had to borrow to meet tax obligations.

After implementing *Guptam Raksha*:

- Moved profit to a hidden mutual fund sweep account.
- Stopped disclosing growth stats.
- Focused on quiet accumulation. Today, his business runs leaner, safer, and is debt-free.

End-of-Chapter Action Steps

- Open a hidden Profit Account with restricted access.
- Remove your Profit Account from financial dashboards.

- Limit profit visibility to key leadership only.
- Avoid showcasing income/profit publicly.
- Conduct internal risk and access audits every quarter.
- Practice silent wealth-building. Let results—not exposure—define your success.

Final Reflection

Your greatest wealth deserves your greatest protection. Chanakya's *Guptam Raksha* is not about hiding—it's about **guarding what you've earned.**

The Profit Maximiser system helps you separate your profit. This sutra helps you protect it. Together, they create an empire of resilience.

In the next chapter, we explore *"Pariksha Karishye"* – the power of examination before trust, and how applying due diligence in financial decisions ensures sustainable profitability.

CHAPTER SEVENTEEN

PARIKSHA KARISHYE – EXAMINE BEFORE YOU TRUST

Sutra Context

"Pariksha Karishye" – One of Chanakya's core mantras, meaning: **"I shall examine first."** In Chanakya's administration, this principle was at the heart of statecraft. Whether appointing ministers, managing spies, or accepting treaties, every decision was preceded by thorough scrutiny.

In business finance, this wisdom urges us to **verify before we trust—especially with money, time, and commitments.** Blind faith in vendors, team members, partnerships, or financial practices without due diligence can result in major losses.

Examine, evaluate, then engage.

Modern Application in Business Finance

Entrepreneurs often:

- Hire quickly without checking financial background or capability.
- Accept partnership terms without understanding the full implications.
- Rely on one source for investment advice.
- Make tax decisions without validating numbers.

Each of these shortcuts can turn into expensive mistakes.

Chanakya reminds us: **Examination is not mistrust. It is smart leadership.**

Profit Maximiser Principle: Trust the System, Verify the Numbers

In the Profit Maximiser framework, consistent checking is a built-in feature:

- Bi-monthly allocations expose how much cash is really available.
- Reviewing each account keeps spending in check.
- Comparing allocation percentages to actual results ensures progress.

By applying *Pariksha Karishye*, you not only implement a system—you **test its integrity regularly.**

How to Practice Financial Diligence in Your Business

Step 1: Audit All Recurring Expenses Every 90 Days

- Create a line-by-line list of all subscriptions, vendor payments, and retainers.
- Ask: *Is this still essential? Is it delivering ROI?*
- Cancel or renegotiate anything not aligned.

Step 2: Reconcile Allocations Every Bi-Monthly Cycle

- On the 10th and 25th:

  ○ Compare allocated vs actual inflow.
  ○ Validate that transfers happened as planned.
  ○ Spot-check one category of expenses for correctness.

Step 3: Validate Every New Proposal or Financial Advice

- Before taking action:

  ○ Ask for documentation.
  ○ Seek at least one alternate opinion.
  ○ Cross-check claims with known data or previous results.

Step 4: Evaluate Performance of Hires and Vendors Using Numbers

- Set 90-day KPIs for every new hire or vendor.
- Review performance based on measurable metrics, not emotions.
- Make renewal or retention decisions only after reviewing results.

Step 5: Review Financial Reports With an Ownership Mindset

- Don't just receive reports—*read* them.
- Ask questions: Why did expenses increase? Are margins trending down?
- Challenge assumptions. Ensure clarity. Then decide.

Business Case Study – Radhika, Founder of a D2C Skincare Brand

Radhika had outsourced her online advertising and logistics to two external vendors. For six months, she paid without questioning.

But when cash flow tightened, she reviewed and found:

- Ad costs were 2X industry standard.
- Logistics vendor was mischarging for returns.

She switched vendors, negotiated new contracts, and recovered ₹7L over two quarters.

She began reviewing every line item monthly, and built a habit of verification into her leadership team.

End-of-Chapter Action Steps

- Audit all expenses and subscriptions this week.
- Reconcile your Profit Maximiser allocations bi-monthly.
- Verify financial advice from at least two sources.
- Create KPI scorecards for vendors and new team members.
- Review one financial report per week in depth.
- Ask "Is this proven?" before every major decision.

Final Reflection

Chanakya's mantra *Pariksha Karishye* is not a sign of distrust—it is a discipline of due diligence.

The Profit Maximiser model gives you structure. But it is your habit of examining, questioning, and validating that will prevent leaks, fraud, and costly errors.

Test the waters. Then set sail. Never before.

CHAPTER EIGHTEEN

DHANAM AGACHATI YATNENA – WEALTH COMES THROUGH EFFORT, NOT LUCK

Sutra Context

"Dhanam Agachati Yatnena" – This ancient teaching of Chanakya translates to: *"Wealth is acquired through effort."* It firmly rejects the illusion of overnight success or the reliance on fortune. Chanakya believed in consistent, intelligent, and persistent effort as the only path to lasting prosperity.

For business owners, this principle is a timely reminder that **no system, tool, or hack can replace focused action and follow-through**. Your profit system may be sound, but it is your disciplined effort that fuels it.

Wealth doesn't arrive by accident. It is engineered by effort.

Modern Application in Business Finance

The allure of passive income, viral launches, or overnight riches is stronger than ever. But most sustainable businesses are built on:

- Consistent client outreach.
- Iterative product improvement.
- Relentless cash flow tracking.
- Daily financial decisions aligned with purpose.

Chanakya's sutra is a powerful mindset: **you are not waiting for wealth, you are working for it.**

Profit Maximiser Principle: Activate the Engine with Effort

The Profit Maximiser model provides the **structure**. Your consistent execution provides the **fuel**. Even the best allocation system is useless if there's no revenue flowing through it.

That means:

- Showing up weekly to market your business.
- Selling regularly—not occasionally.
- Delivering value consistently.
- Reviewing finances on schedule.

Effort isn't about hustle—it's about rhythm. And the Profit Maximiser system makes your financial rhythm count.

How to Align Your Daily Effort with Profit Outcomes
Step 1: Define Your Core Money-Generating Activities

- Identify the top 2–3 tasks that bring in revenue (sales calls, prospecting, delivery).
- Schedule them on your calendar weekly.
- Track time spent vs. income generated.

Step 2: Build a Weekly Profit Workflow

- Set aside time to:

  - Review revenue.
  - Allocate funds to Profit, Tax, Owner's Pay, OPEX.
  - Forecast cash flow.

- Create a checklist and automate it with reminders.

Step 3: Set Monthly Effort-Based KPIs

- Instead of only financial goals, set input goals:

  - **of sales calls made.**
  - **of content pieces published.**
  - **of invoices followed up on.**

- Reward effort consistency, not just results.

Step 4: Eliminate Non-Essential Busywork

- Audit your calendar for low-ROI activities.
- Delegate, automate, or batch non-core work.

- Focus on what drives income and impact.

Step 5: Reframe Challenges as Proof of Commitment

- View delays, rejections, or failures as necessary data.
- Don't shift systems too soon—tune your discipline instead.
- Stay the course for at least 90 days before judging outcomes.

Business Case Study – Anaya, Online Educator
Anaya built a course but saw little traction. She:

- Changed platforms 3 times.
- Tried 5 different pricing strategies.
- Lost motivation quickly.

Then she embraced *Dhanam Agachati Yatnena*:

- Committed to a 90-day content and webinar plan.
- Blocked daily time for outreach and student follow-up.
- Reviewed her Profit Allocations every Friday.

In 4 months, she doubled revenue and built a ₹2L profit buffer.
End-of-Chapter Action Steps

- Identify your top 2–3 income-producing activities.
- Schedule them into your week without fail.
- Create a weekly Profit Workflow checklist.
- Set monthly effort goals (calls, emails, allocations).
- Eliminate 1–2 low-impact tasks this week.
- Stick with your plan for 90 days before pivoting.

Final Reflection

Luck is a bonus. Effort is a guarantee. Chanakya reminds us that **wealth flows where focused energy goes.**

The Profit Maximiser system rewards this effort with structure, predictability, and momentum. By aligning your actions with purpose and rhythm, you turn *Yatna* into *Dhana*—effort into income.

In the next chapter, we explore *"Dhairyam Sarvatra Sadhanam"* – courage as a financial virtue, and how bold decisions made with discipline can multiply your wealth faster than caution ever could.

CHAPTER NINETEEN

DHAIRYAM SARVATRA SADHANAM – COURAGE IS THE KEY TO SUCCESS EVERYWHERE

Sutra Context

"Dhairyam Sarvatra Sadhanam" – Chanakya emphasized that **courage is essential to accomplish anything meaningful.** In the context of finance and business, this sutra reminds us that bold, timely decisions are often the difference between stagnation and success.

Fear of loss, rejection, or uncertainty often paralyzes entrepreneurs. Chanakya urges us to act decisively and boldly—but with wisdom. **Calculated courage, not reckless confidence, drives wealth creation.**

Courage is not the absence of fear; it's action in spite of it.

Modern Application in Business Finance

Many businesses fail to grow because:

- The owner hesitates to increase prices.
- They delay tough cost-cutting decisions.
- They avoid launching offers or making bold asks.
- They underpay themselves out of fear of scarcity.

Financial courage means:

- Pricing with conviction.
- Saying no to unprofitable clients.
- Investing in systems or people that improve profitability.
- Trusting your profit plan—and sticking to it.

Chanakya knew that kingdoms don't expand through hesitation. Businesses don't grow that way either.

Profit Maximiser Principle: Bold Choices Build Profit

The Profit Maximiser system supports courage by creating financial safety nets:

- The Profit Account is your buffer.
- The Owner's Pay Account gives you confidence.
- The OPEX limit forces clarity and prioritization.

These pillars give you the freedom to make bold moves—without fear of total collapse.

How to Exercise Financial Courage in Your Business

Step 1: Raise Your Prices (With Value Alignment)

- Analyze your service or product value.
- Increase prices for the next 3 clients/customers by 10–20%.
- Explain the value confidently—don't apologize.

Step 2: Enforce Payment Discipline

- Refuse delayed payments or poor terms.
- Ask for upfront deposits or milestone-based payments.
- Drop clients who repeatedly delay without valid reasons.

Step 3: Make One Strategic Investment This Quarter

- Choose an investment that could improve revenue or reduce OPEX.
- Examples: Automation software, expert consultant, content team.
- Allocate funds from your Profit or Growth Bucket.

Step 4: Say No More Often

- Review all current clients, tools, and team roles.
- Let go of underperforming assets or obligations.
- Create space for higher-quality opportunities.

Step 5: Trust the Profit Allocations—Even During Lean Months

- Don't stop allocations out of panic.
- Shrink OPEX if needed, but protect Profit and Owner's Pay.
- This builds internal resilience and external stability.

Business Case Study – Pranav, Design Studio Owner

Pranav had a great service but kept underpricing. His cash flow was inconsistent, and team morale was low. After embracing *Dhairyam Sarvatra Sadhanam*:

- He increased project rates by 30%.
- Said no to 2 high-maintenance clients.
- Allocated 15% of each invoice to profit.

Result: Within 6 months, fewer clients, more revenue, and   ₹4.5L in clean profit saved.

End-of-Chapter Action Steps

- Identify one area where you've avoided making a bold decision.
- Raise your price or reject one unfit client this month.
- Make a strategic investment that improves profit leverage.
- Create and enforce a stronger payment policy.
- Trust the system. Stick to your allocations—even in uncertainty.
- Celebrate courageous decisions—even before they yield results.

Final Reflection

Courage builds empires. Chanakya's sutra reminds us that without brave action, no vision becomes reality.

Your Profit Maximiser system is your shield. Use it to step into bolder moves. Every time you act with conviction, you reinforce your financial muscle and expand your earning potential.

In the next chapter, we explore *"Yatha Raja Tatha Praja"* – how the financial habits of the entrepreneur become the culture of the business, and why leading with integrity and discipline creates a prosperous team and company.

91

CHAPTER TWENTY

YATHA RAJA TATHA PRAJA – AS THE LEADER, SO THE PEOPLE

Sutra Context

"Yatha Raja Tatha Praja" – One of Chanakya's most cited political principles, this sutra declares that **the character and conduct of the ruler shapes the conduct of the people**. In business, this translates to a powerful truth: the financial discipline, integrity, and vision of the business owner directly influence the financial behavior and efficiency of the entire team.

Your team mirrors your mindset. Your systems reflect your standards.

When you, as a business owner, operate with accountability, consistency, and clarity, your staff does the same. When you show financial discipline—allocating profits, paying yourself fairly, managing expenses—the culture of financial stewardship flows through the organization.

Modern Application in Business Finance

This principle becomes especially important in small and mid-sized businesses where the founder or owner is often at the financial center of operations. Consider these patterns:

- If the owner delays vendor payments, the team becomes lax with invoicing.
- If salary disbursals are inconsistent, employee loyalty and trust erode.
- If spending is erratic, the team stops caring about budget discipline.

Your team watches and learns from you—**even when you think they aren't.**

Profit Maximiser Principle: Lead Financially by Example

The Profit Maximiser system, when used correctly by the founder, **becomes a model for financial order.** It trains the team to:

- Respect budgets.
- Anticipate allocations.
- Prioritize efficiency over chaos.

When the owner allocates profit first and lives by clear financial rules, it cascades into team behavior—from the accounts desk to the shop floor.

How to Build a Financially Responsible Business Culture

Step 1: Share the Vision, Not the Vault

- Be transparent about the company's financial philosophy (profit-first, lean growth, debt discipline).
- Don't share exact numbers if not necessary—but do share principles.
- Use visual tools like dashboards for revenue goals, cost-saving targets, etc.

Step 2: Pay Salaries and Vendors on Time

- Set an example of punctuality and integrity.
- Automate salary and vendor payments based on OPEX planning.
- Communicate in advance if delays are unavoidable—and avoid them wherever possible.

Step 3: Reward Cost Awareness

- Publicly recognize employees who suggest cost-saving or efficiency ideas.
- Include financial literacy in team training.
- Give quarterly bonuses from profit only when targets are met.

Step 4: Involve Teams in Budget Planning

- Give department heads limited but structured financial authority.
- Review how they track and use budgets.
- This builds accountability and trains leaders internally.

Step 5: Practice What You Preach

- If you're using Profit Maximiser, let your key team members see you:

  - Allocating profits.
  - Taking a regular owner's salary.
  - Saying no to vanity expenses.

- This builds respect and reinforces culture.

Business Case Study – Rajan, Manufacturing Unit Owner

Rajan ran a successful precision engineering workshop with 40 staff. His monthly revenue was ₹30L, but margins were inconsistent, and teams treated raw materials and resources carelessly.

After adopting the Profit Maximiser model and *Yatha Raja Tatha Praja* approach:

- He started allocating 12% to profit and shared the logic with his leadership team.
- Created an employee cost-saving incentive plan.
- Made department heads responsible for tracking their OPEX limits.

Within 8 months, waste dropped by 20%, net margins improved by 6%, and employee satisfaction scores went up.

End-of-Chapter Action Steps

- Share your financial vision and discipline philosophy with your team.
- Pay your people and vendors on time—always.

- Reward team members who protect cash and reduce waste.
- Give teams structured budgets and hold them accountable.
- Review your own consistency—are you living the Profit Maximiser model?
- Build a culture where discipline is admired, not avoided.

Final Reflection

A team follows its leader. If you're financially clear, they will be. If you're financially reactive, so will they.

Chanakya's sutra *Yatha Raja Tatha Praja* is more than a management idea—it's a leadership law. The Profit Maximiser system gives you a powerful way to set that example, turn discipline into culture, and culture into long-term wealth.

In the next chapter, we explore *"Dhanam Agamam Karyam"* – the importance of earning wealth through legitimate means and how ethical profit systems ensure sustainable success and peace of mind.

CHAPTER TWENTY-ONE

DHANAM AGAMAM KARYAM – WEALTH MUST BE EARNED THROUGH LEGITIMATE MEANS

Sutra Context

"Dhanam Agamam Karyam" – Chanakya strongly advocated that **wealth must be acquired through rightful and honest means.** He warned kings against accepting bribes, exploiting subjects, or manipulating revenue

collection. His belief: *Ill-gotten wealth may shine for a moment, but it brings long-term decay.*

In the context of modern business, this means: **ethically earned money is sustainable money**. Revenue built on shady practices, underhanded deals, or manipulation corrodes the business from the inside—even if the numbers look good for a while.

Integrity is the foundation of long-term profitability.

Modern Application in Business Finance

In pursuit of rapid growth or quarterly targets, businesses sometimes:

- Underreport income to avoid taxes.
- Delay vendor payments to hold onto cash.
- Engage in deceptive marketing.
- Exploit labor or environmental loopholes.

While these may provide short-term wins, they compromise brand reputation, employee morale, and legal standing. Chanakya's principle reminds us that **clean money builds powerful legacies**.

Profit Maximiser Principle: Ethics Embedded in Structure

The Profit Maximiser system works best when built on **real, clean revenue**. When all income is accounted for, taxes are pre-allocated, and profit is not derived from deception, the system flows with integrity.

Here's how the system reinforces ethical business:

- A separate Tax Account ensures timely and full compliance.
- Transparent Owner's Pay replaces under-the-table withdrawals.

- Proper vendor payments uphold credibility and trust.

How to Align Profit Systems with Ethical Wealth Creation

Step 1: Declare and Record 100% of Your Revenue

- Avoid under-invoicing, cash transactions, or dual books.
- Record all income in your accounting and tax systems.
- Clean books attract better investors, partners, and peace of mind.

Step 2: Maintain a Dedicated Tax Allocation

- Allocate 15–20% of revenue to a Tax Account.
- Pay taxes before deadlines—avoid interest or penalties.
- Use advisors, not loopholes, to optimize tax legally.

Step 3: Avoid Delayed or Manipulated Payouts

- Pay vendors, staff, and partners within promised timelines.
- Don't use payment delays to stretch cash artificially.
- Integrity in payout creates goodwill and bargaining power.

Step 4: Audit Your Pricing Ethics

- Avoid bait-and-switch tactics, hidden fees, or misleading claims.
- Communicate clearly about what the client is getting.
- Sell only what solves a real problem for them.

Step 5: Create a Whistleblower and Ethics Policy

- Encourage employees to report financial wrongdoing.
- Promote a culture of honesty and financial accountability.
- Ethical transparency can prevent internal fraud or decay.

Business Case Study – Aarti, Owner of a Mid-Sized Packaging Company

Aarti was approached by a large buyer offering ₹1Cr in orders—if she was willing to cut some corners: skip GST, use recycled inferior material, and pay under-the-table to speed up factory clearances.

She refused.

- Chose to build her business slowly, legally, and ethically.
- Used the Profit Maximiser system to stay lean, profitable, and clean.
- Created a transparent tax allocation system and educated her vendors.

Today, her business gets repeat contracts from global eco-friendly brands, and she is invited to speak at ethical sourcing forums.

End-of-Chapter Action Steps

- Ensure 100% revenue is declared in your accounting system.
- Allocate taxes monthly to a separate Tax Account.
- Pay all stakeholders fairly and on time.
- Review your client and vendor agreements for transparency.
- Develop a basic ethics and whistleblower framework.

- Build a brand that is known for doing business the right way.

Final Reflection

Profits earned without principles are poison. Chanakya's *Dhanam Agamam Karyam* is a call to rise above shortcuts and build a legacy of respect.

The Profit Maximiser model gives you the structure to stay ethical. When paired with this sutra, it ensures your wealth is not only abundant—but honorable.

In the next chapter, we explore *"Arthah Yasya Sah Balah"* – true power lies with the one who controls the money—and why business owners must never outsource their financial awareness.

CHAPTER TWENTY-TWO

ARTHAH YASYA SAH BALAH – HE WHO CONTROLS THE MONEY, HOLDS THE POWER

Sutra Context

"Arthah Yasya Sah Balah" – This powerful sutra from Chanakya means: *"He who controls the wealth, holds the power."* It encapsulates a fundamental truth of leadership and influence: **control over money translates to control over decisions, direction, and destiny.**

In ancient times, kings who lost control over treasury operations were manipulated by ministers or enemies. In modern business, owners who are disconnected from their financials lose strategic control—whether to partners, vendors, or even internal teams.

If you don't control your money, someone else will.

Modern Application in Business Finance

Many entrepreneurs:

- Delegate financial oversight too early.
- Avoid reviewing reports and dashboards.
- Trust accountants or staff without clear checks.
- Lose clarity on cash flow, margins, and reserves.

This makes them vulnerable. Financial ignorance, even unintentional, opens the door to embezzlement, poor decisions, or dependency on external advice.

Chanakya urges us to take back control—not to micromanage, but to lead with **financial awareness and command.**

Profit Maximiser Principle: Owner Must Own the Numbers

The Profit Maximiser system isn't just about allocating money—it's about the **owner becoming fluent in money management.**

When you:

- Review allocations every week.
- Understand how much is in each bucket.
- Predict cash flow accurately...

...you build power. You make confident choices. You spot red flags early. You lead.

How to Build Financial Control Without Losing Focus

Step 1: Build a Simple Financial Dashboard

- Use a Google Sheet, dashboard software, or whiteboard to track:

  - Monthly revenue
  - Profit allocation (₹ and %)
  - OPEX spending
  - Tax reserves

- Update every 10th and 25th with allocation days.

Step 2: Set Calendar Alerts for Financial Rituals

- Profit Allocation Days (bi-monthly)
- Monthly financial review (1st week)
- Quarterly strategy & investment review (every 90 days)

Step 3: Learn to Read Your Financial Statements

- Ask your CA or CFO to explain:

  - P&L (Profit & Loss Statement)
  - Balance Sheet
  - Cash Flow Statement

- Watch tutorials or join finance-for-founders workshops.

Step 4: Approve All Major Cash Movements

- No large payment (>₹25K–₹50K) should leave without your review.
- Require explanations or justifications for unusual OPEX spikes.

- Set thresholds for team to act independently, but keep visibility.

Step 5: Use Profit Reviews for Strategic Decisions

- Decide when to invest from profit.
- Choose when to grow, when to cut back.
- Make owner compensation decisions based on trends—not feelings.

Business Case Study – Manish, Co-owner of an Engineering Firm

Manish co-founded an industrial solutions firm with ₹3Cr annual revenue. He focused on delivery while his co-founder handled finance.

When issues emerged:

- Tax dues had been ignored.
- Vendor payments were delayed.
- A staff member had misappropriated ₹4L.

Manish stepped in:

- Implemented the Profit Maximiser system.
- Took over financial review every 15 days.
- Hired a part-time CFO who reported directly to him.

Within 6 months, liabilities were cleared, a ₹9L profit reserve was created, and vendor trust was restored.

End-of-Chapter Action Steps

- Set up a basic financial dashboard for allocations and cash flow.

- Block time for monthly and bi-monthly financial reviews.
- Learn to read and interpret key financial reports.
- Set financial thresholds that require your sign-off.
- Use data to guide hiring, investing, and growth—not gut instinct.
- Never outsource visibility. Keep control without micromanaging.

Final Reflection

Control of finances is control of the business. Chanakya's *Arthah Yasya Sah Balah* reminds us: **your power as a business leader begins with your grip on your money.**

The Profit Maximiser system gives you a method. But it is **your ongoing involvement** that turns that method into a money-making machine.

In the next chapter, we explore *"Dhairyam Samarthyam Karyam"* – how confidence and capability together enable courageous, profitable decisions in business.

CHAPTER TWENTY-THREE

DHAIRYAM SAMARTHYAM KARYAM – COURAGE PLUS CAPABILITY EQUALS PROFITABLE ACTION

Sutra Context

"Dhairyam Samarthyam Karyam" – Chanakya emphasized that **bold action alone is not enough**; it must be backed by **capability, competence, and preparation**. Courage without competence is recklessness. Capability

without courage is wasted potential. But together, they create powerful outcomes.

In a business context, this principle urges entrepreneurs to pair their bold financial goals with solid systems, skilled teams, and strategic thinking. It is **this blend of bravery and readiness** that transforms visions into profits.

Success = Boldness × Readiness.

Modern Application in Business Finance

Too often, businesses:

- Scale before setting up systems.
- Hire in bulk without role clarity.
- Launch offers without testing demand.
- Take financial risks without cash flow buffers.

Chanakya's principle reminds us: **don't just dream—prepare. Don't just act—strengthen.**

Profit Maximiser Principle: Align Bravery with Operational Readiness

The Profit Maximiser system enables you to take calculated, courageous steps:

- Profit accounts build buffers.
- Owner's Pay ensures stability.
- Operating expense limits reveal true efficiency.

With these in place, you can scale, invest, and innovate **from a place of readiness—not desperation.**

How to Combine Boldness with Capability in Business Decisions

Step 1: Set Stretch Goals, But Plan Conservatively

- Dream big with your revenue and profit targets.

- Plan execution with worst-case, realistic-case, and best-case budgets.
- Don't rely on hope—use numbers.

Step 2: Build Capabilities Before Scaling

- Strengthen internal systems: delivery, support, accounting, CRM.
- Train your team for upcoming volume before launching marketing.
- Test offers with a small segment before going public.

Step 3: Use Profit Reserves to Fund Strategic Growth

- Launch new initiatives only if you can fund them from accumulated profit.
- Avoid using operational cash for experimentation.
- This keeps your base business stable while you take calculated risks.

Step 4: Learn Before You Leap

- Attend workshops, speak with mentors, or hire experts before entering new markets or business models.
- Read about financial modeling, pricing, and scalability.
- Use data to inform bold decisions—not just gut feeling.

Step 5: Measure Bold Moves Against Business Capability Score

- Rate your business 1–5 in the following:

  - Team Strength

- ◦ Financial Stability
- ◦ Systems & Processes
- ◦ Market Demand Knowledge
- ◦ Operational Efficiency

- Don't act unless your average score is 3.5 or above.

Business Case Study – Priya, Chemical Products Manufacturer

Priya wanted to expand her business by launching an eco-friendly cleaning line. The opportunity was exciting, and competitors were few.

Instead of jumping in:

- She conducted a customer pilot across 20 distributors.
- Used ₹5L from her profit account for branding and certification.
- Scaled internal QA processes and logistics before expansion.

Within 10 months, the new line contributed 35% to revenue with higher margins—and zero debt.

End-of-Chapter Action Steps

- Set bold goals—but support them with conservative execution plans.
- Conduct a business capability audit before major initiatives.
- Use accumulated profits—not borrowed funds—for innovation.
- Build internal capacity (team, systems, finance) before scaling.
- Pair every bold move with a risk mitigation plan.

- Evaluate all moves against the Courage × Capability equation.

Final Reflection

Chanakya's wisdom guides us beyond just bravery. It tells us to pair every courageous decision with strong preparation.

The Profit Maximiser model makes your business ready. This sutra gives you the courage to act. Together, they position you for bold, sustained, and ethical growth.

In the next chapter, we explore *"Sampadam Sahanubhuti Karyam"* – how the conscious use of wealth not only supports personal and business goals but uplifts others and builds a legacy.

CHAPTER TWENTY-FOUR

SAMPADAM SAHANUBHUTI KARYAM – WEALTH MUST SERVE A PURPOSE BEYOND THE SELF

Sutra Context

"Sampadam Sahanubhuti Karyam" – This lesser-known but profound extension of Chanakya's philosophy means: **"Wealth must be used with empathy."** In ancient texts and political strategy, Chanakya often advised that true prosperity lies not just in accumulating wealth, but in **applying it mindfully**—for personal well-being, collective growth, and societal good.

Wealth, if hoarded or flaunted without purpose, becomes stagnant and even corrosive. But when used with empathy and foresight, it becomes a tool for **transformation and legacy-building.**

Wealth multiplies when it's aligned with purpose.

Modern Application in Business Finance

Entrepreneurs are often focused on profit targets, scaling goals, and owner's wealth. But without a higher purpose, financial success can feel hollow and unstable. Businesses that survive long-term often:

- Serve beyond their own needs.
- Create livelihoods.
- Solve real problems.
- Reinforce values in their ecosystem.

This chapter emphasizes a critical truth: **your profit must have a purpose beyond your pocket.**

Chanakya believed a wise king reinvested wealth in the well-being of his people. Similarly, a wise entrepreneur uses profit to uplift not just themselves, but their team, community, and customers.

Profit Maximiser Principle: Purpose-Led Allocation Multiplies Value

The Profit Maximiser system encourages you to intentionally direct your surplus—first to **yourself**, and then to those around you:

- Pay yourself to be stable.
- Reinvest in systems to grow sustainably.
- Uplift others to build a legacy.

This flow ensures that **profit isn't just protected—it's purposeful.**

How to Integrate Purpose into Profit

Step 1: Define Your Wealth Impact Vision

- Ask: *What is my money for?*
- Examples: Providing employment, mentoring young entrepreneurs, supporting local education, donating to causes.
- Write down 3 values your financial decisions must honor.

Step 2: Allocate a Fixed % of Profit for Purposeful Impact

- Create a "Legacy Allocation" bucket: 5–10% of quarterly profits.
- Use it for:

  - Team development (bonuses, training).
  - Community support (education, health drives).
  - Environmental responsibility (sustainable sourcing, recycling).

Step 3: Make Team Well-being a Line Item

- Fund professional development programs.
- Sponsor health, insurance, or emergency support.
- Celebrate milestones and build team culture.

Step 4: Fund Purpose-Led Innovation

- Launch new products or services that solve meaningful problems.
- Use retained profits to enter impact sectors (health, education, sustainability).

- Create access initiatives (scholarships, sliding-scale pricing, rural outreach).

Step 5: Share Your Success With Integrity

- Highlight the impact your business has made—not just your revenue.
- Inspire others in your ecosystem to blend profit with purpose.
- Stay grounded—let impact be quiet, deep, and consistent.

Business Case Study – Arun, Owner of a Steel Fabrication Unit

Arun's business generated ₹80L profit in a strong year. Earlier, he would reinvest all of it into expanding operations.

After reflecting on *Sampadam Sahanubhuti Karyam*, he:

- Created a ₹5L education fund for children of factory workers.
- Sponsored skill training programs in welding and safety.
- Provided performance-linked profit sharing to employees.

Result: Employee retention improved by 35%, absenteeism dropped, and clients began referring his company as an ethical vendor.

The impact also enhanced his brand story—making him eligible for larger, government-aligned projects.

End-of-Chapter Action Steps

- Define your financial purpose beyond survival and growth.
- Set up a Legacy Allocation or Impact Fund from quarterly profits.
- Review how much your financial decisions align with your core values.
- Invest in people—your team, your suppliers, your community.
- Identify 1 area of your business that can solve a deeper problem.
- Communicate your impact with humility and authenticity.

Final Reflection

Wealth without wisdom becomes vanity. Profit without purpose becomes pressure. But **wealth applied with empathy creates power and peace.**

Chanakya's *Sampadam Sahanubhuti Karyam* reminds us that business success is not complete until it uplifts others.

The Profit Maximiser system shows you where your money is going. This sutra shows you **why** it should go there.

In the next chapter, we explore *"Lakshya Spashtam Karyam"* – the principle of clarity in financial goals and direction, and how your business decisions sharpen when your financial vision is precise.

CHAPTER TWENTY-FIVE

LAKSHYA SPASHTAM KARYAM – CLARITY OF FINANCIAL VISION DRIVES STRATEGIC ACTION

Sutra Context

"Lakshya Spashtam Karyam" – This strategic maxim drawn from the core of Chanakya's advisory approach emphasizes: **"Actions must be driven by clear goals."** Without a defined destination, even the most diligent

activity loses direction. Chanakya insisted that leaders operate not just with energy but with exactness.

For entrepreneurs and business owners, this translates into an essential discipline: **clarity in financial goals, resource allocations, and wealth vision is non-negotiable.** Every rupee must have a role, every decision a destination.

Where clarity ends, chaos begins.

Modern Application in Business Finance

In today's complex business environment, many entrepreneurs operate reactively:

- Revenue targets change month to month.
- Investments are made impulsively without ROI planning.
- Team expenses balloon due to vague budgeting.
- Owner's Pay is inconsistent.

Without financial clarity, businesses drift. Profits vanish. Cash flow tightens. And decisions are made under pressure rather than with purpose.

Chanakya's teaching urges us to flip this script: **clarity must precede commitment.**

Profit Maximiser Principle: Systemic Clarity Creates Profitable Discipline

The Profit Maximiser system functions as a financial compass—it divides revenue into clearly defined buckets:

- Profit
- Tax
- Owner's Pay
- Operating Expenses

When paired with **clear financial goals**, this system becomes a power tool:

- You know what you're working toward.
- You know how much each bucket needs.
- You spot deviations early—and adjust confidently.

**How to Sharpen Financial Clarity in Your Business
Step 1: Define Your 12-Month Financial North Star**

- Set a **Revenue Target** (e.g., ₹1.2Cr/year).
- Set a **Net Profit Target** (e.g., 20% = ₹24L).
- Set an **Owner's Pay Target** (e.g., ₹80K/month minimum).
- Write these where you can see them weekly.

Step 2: Reverse-Engineer Monthly Allocations

- Break annual targets into monthly milestones.
- Use your TAPs (Target Allocation Percentages) to calculate monthly:

  - How much goes into Profit?
  - What are your ideal OPEX limits?
  - How much must you allocate to tax to stay compliant?

Step 3: Identify Key Financial Focus Areas Each Quarter

- Focus areas could include:

  - Reducing OPEX from 50% to 40%.

- ◦ Increasing Owner's Pay.
- ◦ Growing profit reserves by ₹2L.

- Keep only **one main financial goal per quarter** for team alignment.

Step 4: Visualize Cash Flow with Clarity Tools

- Use tools like:

  - ◦ Google Sheets with monthly dashboards.
  - ◦ Accounting software with visual insights (e.g., Zoho Books, QuickBooks).
  - ◦ Printed cash flow trackers in team areas (for small businesses).

Step 5: Make Weekly Decisions Aligned to the Financial Vision

- Ask weekly: *Does this decision support or dilute my goal?*
- Delay decisions that don't directly support your quarterly focus.
- Communicate your vision during team meetings and strategic huddles.

Business Case Study – Kavita, Owner of a Regional Textile Brand

Kavita was running a profitable but chaotic retail operation with ₹1.5Cr annual revenue. Her issue:

- Staff bonuses were ad hoc.
- Inventory overruns impacted margins.
- Owner's Pay fluctuated wildly.

After implementing *Lakshya Spashtam Karyam*:

- She set a clear 1-year vision: ₹2Cr revenue, ₹30L profit, ₹1L/month salary.
- Used TAPs to track weekly allocations and built dashboards with her bookkeeper.
- Adjusted discounts, optimized inventory, and paused non-core spending.

Within 9 months, she hit 92% of her target—and doubled her quarterly profit distribution.

End-of-Chapter Action Steps

- Write down your 12-month revenue, profit, and Owner's Pay targets.
- Set monthly allocation goals using the Profit Maximiser structure.
- Choose 1 key financial improvement for the next quarter.
- Build a simple dashboard to track progress.
- Review all financial decisions weekly through the lens of your stated vision.
- Share the vision with your leadership team—make it everyone's goal.

Final Reflection

Chanakya believed that **vague intentions weaken strategy**. Without clarity, even the best systems lose effectiveness.

The Profit Maximiser model is your structure. *Lakshya Spashtam Karyam* is your compass. When paired, they create a business that operates with precision, discipline, and conviction.

In the next chapter, we will explore *"Anagatam Bhayam Drishtva Yojanam Kurute Budhah"* – the principle of preparing financially for future threats, and how proactive planning keeps your profit safe even in turbulent times.

CHAPTER TWENTY-SIX

ANAGATAM BHAYAM DRISHTVA YOJANAM KURUTE BUDHAH – PREPARE FOR UNSEEN FINANCIAL THREATS WITH STRATEGIC FORESIGHT

Sutra Context

"Anagatam Bhayam Drishtva Yojanam Kurute Budhah" – This farsighted principle of Chanakya translates as: **"The wise prepare for dangers not yet seen."** Unlike reactive leaders, the truly strategic ones scan the horizon, anticipate risks, and put systems in place before adversity strikes.

In personal and business finance, this is the difference between surviving a crisis and collapsing under it. Entrepreneurs who succeed long-term are those who build **resilience proactively—not as a response, but as a principle.**

What you prepare for, rarely destroys you. What you ignore, almost always does.

Modern Application in Business Finance

Many businesses falter due to predictable but unprepared risks:

- Client payments get delayed.
- Raw material costs spike.
- Economic cycles shift.
- Regulatory changes force sudden compliance burdens.

Chanakya reminds us: these are not surprises—they're **eventualities**. The wise entrepreneur does not wait to respond. They allocate, buffer, and insulate before the storm.

Profit Maximiser Principle: Build a Fortress Before the Fire

The Profit Maximiser system, when implemented with this sutra, becomes a resilience tool:

- The Profit Account becomes a war chest.
- The Tax Account prevents last-minute scrambling.
- The Emergency Fund shields from cash flow shocks.

This setup ensures that no single event can wipe out your business—or your peace of mind.

How to Prepare Financially for the Unseen

Step 1: Build an Emergency Buffer (Business + Personal)

- Allocate 5–10% of revenue monthly until you build:

  - **3–6 months of Operating Expenses** in a Business Emergency Account.
  - **6 months of Personal Expenses** from Owner's Pay into a Personal Buffer.

- Keep these in separate, interest-earning, liquid instruments (e.g., sweep-in FDs, liquid mutual funds).

Step 2: Simulate Worst-Case Scenarios Annually

- Imagine:

  - Revenue drops by 30%.
  - A top-paying client defaults.
  - An economic slowdown lasts 6 months.

- What would you cut? What would you preserve? Document a response plan.

Step 3: Create a 'Slow Season Survival Plan'

- For seasonal businesses or B2B firms:

  - Chart when revenue dips annually.
  - Save in advance from peak months to carry you through.
  - Consider cutting recurring but delayable costs temporarily.

Step 4: Maintain a Crisis Allocation from Profit

- From your quarterly profit share, assign 10–20% to a "Future Risk" vault.
- Use only in cases of:

  - Legal penalties
  - Sudden loss of working capital
  - Health crisis affecting business continuity

Step 5: Develop Redundancy in Revenue

- Identify your top 3 revenue streams.
- Aim to reduce overdependence on one stream (no more than 40%).
- Explore adjacent income opportunities (consulting, digital products, bulk orders).

Business Case Study – Gaurav, Export Furniture Manufacturer

Gaurav exported wooden furniture to Europe and the Middle East. In 2020, a logistics crisis delayed shipments by 90 days.

Many peers went bankrupt. But Gaurav had:

- 4 months of OPEX in reserves.
- Insurance on receivables.
- A second line of domestic institutional clients.

He weathered the storm, paid his staff without layoffs, and grew 18% the following year.

End-of-Chapter Action Steps

- Start an Emergency Fund for both business and personal life.
- Simulate 3 worst-case scenarios and prepare response playbooks.
- Create a slow season cash flow buffer strategy.
- Assign 10–20% of quarterly profit to future risk vaults.
- Diversify revenue streams to avoid single-source dependence.
- Review and rehearse your plan annually like a financial fire drill.

Final Reflection

Survival is not accidental—it is strategic. Chanakya's *Anagatam Bhayam Drishtva Yojanam Kurute Budhah* reminds us that fortune favors the financially foresighted.

The Profit Maximiser structure is not just about thriving in the good times. It is a system built for **survival, recovery, and long-term dominance**—when implemented with wisdom and war-like preparation.

In the next chapter, we'll explore *"Kalabhedam Jnatva Karyam"* – the art of timing in financial decisions, and how smart entrepreneurs use seasons and cycles to their advantage rather than fighting them blindly.

CHAPTER TWENTY-SEVEN

KALABHEDAM JNATVA KARYAM – TIMING IS STRATEGY: MASTERING BUSINESS AND FINANCIAL CYCLES

Sutra Context

"Kalabhedam Jnatva Karyam" – Chanakya emphasized that the **understanding of timing is essential before taking action.** His advice to kings was not just to act, but to act at the right time. A move made too soon invites disaster;

a delay can mean missed opportunity. Wise leadership is not just about courage or planning—it's about *timing*.

In today's business environment, this ancient wisdom remains profoundly relevant. The ability to **recognize seasons, economic cycles, market trends, and personal readiness** is the hallmark of sustainable financial leadership.

Good decisions made at the wrong time yield poor results. Great leaders wait—and strike.

Modern Application in Business Finance

Many businesses fail not because their idea was wrong, but because their timing was:

- Scaling up during a market downturn.
- Launching new products without buyer readiness.
- Investing surplus during peak pricing cycles.
- Hiring before demand stabilizes.

Chanakya's sutra teaches us that **the wise act only after understanding the rhythms of time.** Financial success comes not just from effort—but from knowing *when* to apply it.

Profit Maximiser Principle: Match Financial Rhythm with Business Cycles

The Profit Maximiser framework encourages *fixed financial discipline*, but also demands *flexible strategic awareness*.

It works best when allocations and reinvestment decisions are adjusted to suit:

- Seasonal patterns
- Economic cycles
- Industry phases

- Internal business maturity

It teaches you to act boldly *only when the timing supports it*—and to pause, build buffers, or consolidate when timing does not.

How to Apply Strategic Timing in Financial Decisions
Step 1: Study Your Business Seasonality

- Identify when revenue peaks and drops:

  - Monthly
  - Quarterly
  - Yearly (festivals, monsoons, financial year-end)

- Align large marketing pushes, inventory buying, and hiring with peak seasons.
- Save more aggressively in off-peak periods.

Step 2: Align Big Moves with Economic Trends

- Before launching new ventures:

  - Study GDP, interest rate, and inflation trends.
  - Watch industry data: new regulations, tech shifts, demand contractions.
  - Time capital investments during economic expansions—not contractions.

Step 3: Delay Gratification During Instability

- During uncertain periods (e.g., elections, pandemics, policy shakeups):

- ◦ Reduce risky OPEX.
- ◦ Postpone ambitious expansions.
- ◦ Focus on customer retention and lean delivery.

Step 4: Use Profit Reserves to Leap at the Right Moment

- When opportunity knocks:

  - ◦ Use accumulated profit—not borrowed funds—to capitalize.
  - ◦ Strike when competitors are hesitant.
  - ◦ Move first, but only when **you're financially ready and the market is right.**

Step 5: Create a 3-Level Timing Matrix

Timing Type	Good Time to Act	Actions to Prioritize
Business Season	Peak sales months, product launch windows	Sales blitz, hiring, reinvestment
Market Cycle	Economic expansion, rising demand	R&D, scaling, pricing updates
Internal Timing	Profit reserves high, team well-aligned, delivery ready	Asset buying, new markets, bonuses

Business Case Study – Sheetal, Co-owner of a Hospitality Chain

Sheetal was planning a major renovation of her two resort properties. Aesthetically and functionally, it made sense. But it was 2021—tourism was still recovering post-lockdown.

She waited. Saved. Observed.

By early 2023:

- Tourism surged.
- Construction costs dropped.
- Competitors were still recovering.

She used her　 ₹20L profit reserve and timed the launch ahead of the summer boom.

Result: She was 3X overbooked, became a preferred partner on top platforms, and grew her valuation by 40% in 6 months.

End-of-Chapter Action Steps

- Map your business's revenue seasonality and align decisions accordingly.
- Study external macro indicators before making major investments.
- Avoid overexpansion during volatile or unclear market phases.
- Create a timing checklist before any capital decision.
- Delay unnecessary gratification in slow cycles—optimize instead.
- Act with boldness only when internal strength and external timing align.

Final Reflection

Knowing *when not to act* is as powerful as knowing *when to act*. Chanakya's *Kalabhedam Jnatva Karyam* is a reminder that **timing is not luck—it is learned, tracked, and obeyed.**

The Profit Maximiser system helps you build strength. But Chanakya's timing principle ensures that your strength is applied with precision—leading to lasting wealth, not just short-term wins.

In the next chapter, we'll explore *"Sanchita Sampada Raksha Karyam"* – the art of protecting accumulated wealth from erosion, temptation, and premature use.

133

SANCHITA SAMPADA RAKSHA KARYAM – PROTECTING ACCUMULATED WEALTH FROM EROSION AND EMOTIONAL DECISIONS

Sutra Context

"Sanchita Sampada Raksha Karyam" – This timeless lesson from Chanakya's philosophy focuses on a simple but

often neglected truth: **wealth once accumulated must be vigilantly protected.**

Accumulated wealth is not just the fruit of effort—it is the foundation of future opportunity. But just as a granary left unguarded can be eaten by rats, **profits and reserves not shielded with structure and intention can vanish.**

Chanakya understood that unprotected wealth invites three threats:

1. External misuse (fraud, theft, bad partnerships)
2. Internal impulse (emotional decisions, ego spending)
3. Structural erosion (inflation, misallocation, untracked use)

Wealth is not truly yours until it is guarded from misuse—by others and by yourself.

Modern Application in Business Finance

Businesses accumulate capital—then lose it by:

• Tapping into profit reserves for short-term desires.
• Lending without contracts or strategy.
• Making emotional investments due to peer pressure.
• Lacking clarity on reinvestment timing.

This creates a dangerous pattern: earn → save → misuse → start over.

Chanakya advises a different cycle: **earn → protect → grow → secure → serve.**

Profit Maximiser Principle: Guard the Vault Before You Grow It

The Profit Maximiser system creates a protected vault (your Profit Account). But unless you actively safeguard it:

- You may dip into it during low-energy or ego-driven moments.
- You may use it for validation purchases instead of value investments.
- You may deploy it prematurely without ROI clarity.

To follow Chanakya's advice, your Profit Vault must be:

- Separated
- Strategically governed
- Grown only after it's fully protected

How to Protect Accumulated Wealth in Business
Step 1: Create "Do Not Touch" Rules for Your Profit Vault

- Profit withdrawals are permitted **only quarterly** after performance review.
- Use the 50/50 rule:

  - 50% for reinvestment or personal growth.
  - 50% retained to grow core reserves.

- In low-profit quarters: delay withdrawal, do not dip into reserves.

Step 2: Move Wealth Out of Operational Visibility

- Transfer part of your profit reserves into:

  - Business fixed deposits
  - Low-risk mutual funds
  - Debt instruments

- Keep these outside your primary business banking platform.
- Make access friction high (e.g., manual withdrawal, co-signatory).

Step 3: Establish a Wealth Guardrail SOP

- Write down when profit **can** and **cannot** be used.
- Examples:

  - OK: Expansion into a proven vertical.
  - Not OK: Buying a vanity office or vehicle.

- Share this framework with your co-founders, financial advisor, or CFO.

Step 4: Build an Annual Profit Deployment Calendar

- January: Profit audit + vault reinforcement
- April & October: Profit disbursement windows (aligned with tax planning)
- July: Mid-year reinvestment review
- December: Impact allocation (e.g., CSR, team bonuses, personal wealth planning)

Step 5: Identify and Control Personal Spending Triggers

- Recognize when you spend:

  - To reward stress (emotional reward)
  - To show status (ego validation)
  - Because others are doing it (comparison pressure)

- Replace with alternate reward rituals that don't drain your reserves

    ◦ e.g., experience bonuses, wellness travel, or symbolic celebrations

Business Case Study – Imran, Owner of an Auto Components Manufacturing Unit

Imran grew his business steadily for 6 years and saved ₹40L in accumulated profit. But in year 7:

- He impulsively funded his cousin's startup with ₹20L.
- Bought a new SUV and upgraded office interiors.
- Delayed key equipment maintenance.

By year-end:

- His reserves were down to ₹6L.
- Productivity dropped.
- He had to take a ₹15L business loan to plug cash flow gaps.

After embracing *Sanchita Sampada Raksha Karyam*:

- He moved profit to a fixed-income vault.
- Created quarterly disbursement rules.
- Funded future investments only from surplus, not from reserves.

Today, his reserve stands at ₹58L, his profit use is strategic, and he sleeps soundly—even during downturns.

End-of-Chapter Action Steps

- Set up quarterly rules for profit withdrawal and usage.
- Transfer part of your reserve to low-risk, off-platform instruments.
- Write and follow a "Wealth Guardrail SOP."
- Track and manage emotional spending patterns—personally and professionally.
- Create a profit calendar that balances reinforcement, rewards, and reinvestment.
- Always remember: you're not rich by what you earn, but by what you *protect*.

Final Reflection

Chanakya's brilliance lay not in his ability to help kings earn wealth—but in his insistence that they **defend** it.

The same applies to you. Your reserves are your fortress. Protect them—**from temptation, emotion, and poor judgment.**

The Profit Maximiser framework is your lock. This sutra is your watchtower.

In the next chapter, we conclude with *"Arthasya Antyam Sadhanam Dharma"* – how true wealth is realized only when aligned with purpose, values, and service beyond self.

ARTHASYA ANTYAM SADHANAM DHARMA – WEALTH'S FINAL PURPOSE IS RIGHTEOUS USE

Sutra Context

"Arthasya Antyam Sadhanam Dharma" – One of Chanakya's most philosophical sutras, this translates to: **"The ultimate purpose of wealth is to serve dharma."**

Dharma here refers not just to religious or spiritual duty, but to **righteousness, responsibility, and legacy.** Chanakya believed that **wealth without dharma is dangerous, and dharma without wealth is powerless.** True financial mastery lies in using money to align with your deeper purpose—and to serve something greater than yourself.

This chapter concludes our journey by anchoring every action, structure, and strategy of the Profit Maximiser system into something more powerful: *meaning*.

Wealth is the vehicle. Dharma is the destination.

Modern Application in Business Finance

In a competitive world, it's easy to become obsessed with net worth, revenue targets, and scale. But wealth without values breeds:

- Greed
- Exploitation
- Emptiness
- Stress masked as success

Chanakya reminds us that the **true measure of wealth is not what it buys, but what it builds.** Does your profit create peace? Growth? Opportunity? Impact?

Businesses that last beyond generations are built not just on systems—but on *soul*.

Profit Maximiser Principle: Wealth with Values Multiplies Legacy

The Profit Maximiser model helps you:

- Earn consistently
- Protect reserves
- Grow sustainably
- Reward yourself fairly

But it becomes truly transformational when you use it to:

- Fund impact
- Support causes
- Elevate communities
- Pass on wisdom, not just money

Wealth with values becomes wealth that lives on.
How to Align Your Wealth with Dharma
Step 1: Define Your Financial Dharma

- Ask:

  - Why do I want to grow wealth?
  - Who will benefit from my profit?
  - What do I want my business to stand for?

- Write a one-paragraph personal Wealth Dharma
  Statement.

Step 2: Allocate for Purpose-Driven Giving

- From your quarterly profit, dedicate 5–10% toward
  impact:

  - Community upliftment
  - Education scholarships
  - Environmental responsibility
  - Support for employees in need

- Ensure your giving is consistent, not just seasonal or
  emotional.

Step 3: Build a Purpose Fund (Legacy Vault)

- Set aside part of annual profit in a long-term fund:

  - Philanthropic corpus
  - Foundation fund
  - Endowment for future entrepreneurs

- This vault must grow like any other asset.

Step 4: Run Your Business as a Dharma-Aligned Enterprise

- Treat your employees with dignity.
- Practice transparent pricing.
- Deliver real value.
- Pay taxes with pride, not reluctance.

Step 5: Teach Financial Dharma to the Next Generation

- Share your Profit Maximiser journey with family and team.
- Involve children, heirs, and mentees in wealth creation with values.
- Make your balance sheet a lesson—not a secret.

Business Case Study – Seema, Co-founder of an IT Services Company

Seema ran a successful IT consultancy with ₹3.5Cr in annual revenue. After hitting personal financial goals, she asked: *Now what?*

That question led her to:

- Start a technical training program for underprivileged youth.
- Allocate ₹5L annually from her profit reserve toward scholarships.
- Mentor 3 young women entrepreneurs every year.

In 5 years, her company became not just profitable—but purposeful. Employee retention rose, clients referred her ethically driven model, and Seema found joy in impact.

End-of-Chapter Action Steps

- Define and write your Financial Dharma Statement.
- Allocate 5–10% of profit toward a cause that aligns with your values.
- Create a Legacy Vault to fund long-term impact.
- Make purpose a visible part of your business culture.
- Mentor or uplift someone through your financial and business wisdom.
- Remember: **wealth is a tool. Dharma gives it direction.**

Final Reflection

Chanakya ends where all wise paths must end: **in meaning.**

We've built structures. Allocated funds. Protected reserves. Grown wealth. But unless that wealth *serves*, it simply sits.

With *Arthasya Antyam Sadhanam Dharma*, you turn your Profit Maximiser system into a life-guiding tool—one that brings not just profit, but peace.

Let your wealth be wise. Let it be well-earned. Let it be well-used. Let it be a force not just for your prosperity—but for the world's betterment.

This is true wealth. This is dharma. This is legacy.

CHAPTER THIRTY

SHUBHASYA SHEEGHRAM – TAKE SWIFT ACTION ON WHAT IS RIGHTEOUS AND TIMELY

Sutra Context

"Shubhasya Sheeghram" – A popular Sanskrit maxim meaning **"Act swiftly on good intentions."** While not directly from Chanakya's Arthashastra, it aligns perfectly with his strategic philosophy. Chanakya often warned against delays in action once clarity is achieved, especially in matters of governance, finance, and leadership.

This sutra reminds us: **once you know what is right, delay becomes the enemy.** In the context of business finance, once we know what builds wealth, protects reserves, and aligns with dharma—we must act decisively and swiftly.

The longer you delay the right action, the more power you give to inertia and fear.

Modern Application in Business Finance

Many entrepreneurs stay stuck in loops:

- They know they need to raise prices—but delay.
- They know a team restructure is needed—but hesitate.
- They want to implement Profit Maximiser—but wait for the "perfect month."

Inaction becomes expensive. Clarity without execution leads to wasted potential and even financial setbacks.

Chanakya would advise: *"If you have built clarity, act now. If you have clarity and don't act, you are sabotaging your own strategy."*

Profit Maximiser Principle: Speed of Implementation Unlocks Value

The Profit Maximiser system is a blueprint. But its power lies in **doing**, not just knowing. This final operational pillar says: once you understand the method, **don't wait to implement.**

Here's what happens when you act fast:

- You build confidence.
- You see immediate financial improvement (even at 1% allocation).
- You overcome perfectionism.
- You create momentum.

Waiting weakens wisdom. Action multiplies mastery.

How to Act Swiftly on Financial Wisdom

Step 1: Set a 7-Day Rule for All Financial Clarity

- When a financial decision makes sense:

  - Pricing change
  - Hiring/firing call
  - Launch or kill a product

- Act within 7 days or calendar the decision.

Step 2: Begin Profit Maximiser at 1% This Week

- Open 3 new accounts (Profit, Tax, Owner's Pay).
- Start by allocating just 1% to each bucket.
- Scale from there monthly.
- The first step creates the shift.

Step 3: Audit the 'Clarity Backlog'

- List 5 financial decisions you've delayed despite knowing they're right.
- Assign a deadline to each.
- Commit to executing at least 2 in the next 15 days.

Step 4: Install a Monthly Action Review Ritual

- Every 1st or 7th of the month:

  - What new decision was implemented?
  - What clarity didn't lead to action?
  - Why?

- ○ What's your next move?

Step 5: Create a Bias Toward Action Culture

- Celebrate team members who act with clarity.
- Make speed of responsible implementation a performance metric.
- Set timelines shorter than industry average for internal deployments.

Business Case Study – Mahesh, Founder of a SaaS Company

Mahesh knew his monthly churn was rising. He had clarity that better onboarding and a feedback loop would help—but waited 4 months trying to perfect the experience.

During that time, he lost ₹12L in predictable MRR loss.

After adopting *Shubhasya Sheeghram:*

- Launched a minimum viable onboarding with a 15-minute welcome call.
- Added a feedback form with just 3 questions.
- Implemented Profit Maximiser with 3% allocation instantly.

Churn reduced by 18% in 45 days, and he created ₹ 3.2L in profit reserves within 3 months.

End-of-Chapter Action Steps

- Make 1% Profit Maximiser allocations this week—no excuses.

- List 5 delayed financial decisions and schedule action dates.
- Set a 7-day rule for all clarity-based decisions.
- Begin a monthly action audit ritual with your team or coach.
- Build a reputation for timely, ethical, and bold execution.
- Remember: **it's not just what you know. It's how fast you act once you know.**

Final Reflection

Chanakya ends where implementation begins: **decisive action.**

Every chapter in this book has given you sutra-based financial clarity. Now, the only thing left to do is **act.**

Don't wait for perfection. Don't wait for more comfort. Don't wait for permission. You are the ruler of your financial kingdom. *Act like it.*

With *Shubhasya Sheeghram*, you become the entrepreneur who leads with wisdom, builds with speed, and leaves behind not just wealth—but a legacy of action.

Clarity is a gift. Speed is your duty. Impact is the result.

Dridh Sankalpah Lakshya Siddhi – Firm Resolve is the Foundation of Financial Success

Sutra Context

"Dridh Sankalpah Lakshya Siddhi" – This Sanskrit sutra means: **"Firm resolve leads to goal achievement."** Chanakya, in both his writings and governance strategies, emphasized unwavering determination as the bedrock of long-term success.

In the context of wealth, business, and cash flow management, this principle teaches us that once you commit to a vision—be it building reserves, optimizing cash flow, or growing legacy wealth—you must **resolve to stay the course** through distraction, temptation, and setbacks.

The strength of your commitment shapes the stability of your wealth.

Modern Application in Business Finance

In a world of fast results and instant gratification, business owners often:

- Quit systems that don't yield results in 30 days.
- Abandon financial discipline during sales slumps.
- Change strategies too often, confusing their teams.

This leads to an unstable financial foundation. Chanakya's wisdom is clear: **commit once—refine along the way—but never waver.**

Profit Maximiser Principle: Stay Consistent to See Compounding Results

The Profit Maximiser system only works when used **with discipline over time**. The power of:

- 1% allocations
- Bi-monthly financial rituals
- Quarterly reviews

...is not in the technique alone, but in **relentless repetition**. Chanakya would say: if you've chosen a wise path, don't look back. **Refine the journey, don't change the destination.**

How to Practice Financial Resolve in Your Business

Step 1: Set a 12-Month Non-Negotiable Financial Commitment

- Examples:

  - "I will make Profit Allocations every 10th and 25th, regardless of revenue."
  - "I will not borrow for indulgence."
  - "I will pay myself a fixed Owner's Pay each month."

- Share your commitment with an accountability partner or advisor.

Step 2: Use Micro-Tracking for Macro Discipline

- Keep a journal or dashboard to track monthly:

  - Allocations made
  - Owner's Pay received
  - Profit Vault balance
  - OPEX vs Revenue trend

- Seeing progress reinforces your resolve.

Step 3: Reinforce Your Vision Quarterly

- Re-read your Wealth Dharma Statement (see Chapter 22).
- Conduct quarterly financial reviews, not just P&L analysis but *values check-ins.*
- Ask: Are your financial habits honoring your vision?

Step 4: Resist the Urge to Pivot When It's Working

- Don't reduce allocations because revenue dipped—reduce OPEX.

- Don't skip rituals because of busy schedules—protect your rhythm.
- Review and reflect, but hold firm to the foundation.

Step 5: Ritualize Your Commitment

- Morning affirmation: *"I am a disciplined steward of my wealth."*
- Weekly reflection: What did I protect? What did I compromise?
- Annual recommitment ceremony: make it symbolic and sacred.

Business Case Study – Nishita, Owner of an Organic Food Startup

Nishita began using Profit Maximiser at a time when she was barely breaking even. Her initial allocations were just ₹1,000 per account.

She was tempted to pause the system multiple times—when orders dropped, during vendor delays, or when expansion opportunities arose. But she stayed committed.

Today:

- Her Profit Vault stands at ₹18L.
- She pays herself ₹75K/month consistently.
- She's never delayed staff salary in 3 years.

Her brand is not only financially stable but culturally admired.

End-of-Chapter Action Steps

- Declare a 12-month non-negotiable financial resolution.

- Track your progress weekly or monthly.
- Ritualize your commitment with personal and team reminders.
- Hold the line during tough quarters—cut costs, not discipline.
- Celebrate consistency as much as growth.
- Remember: **the strongest systems fail without resolve. The simplest systems thrive with it.**

Final Reflection

The final quality that makes the Profit Maximiser system work is not intelligence. It's not talent. It's **discipline with time**.

With *Dridh Sankalpah Lakshya Siddhi*, you become unshakable. You become the kind of entrepreneur who not only earns—but sustains, scales, and serves.

Let the world chase quick wins. You'll build enduring wealth. One allocation, one habit, one choice at a time.

Resolve is the real currency of long-term success.

Implementing Profit Maximiser — A provide yourself first cashflow management

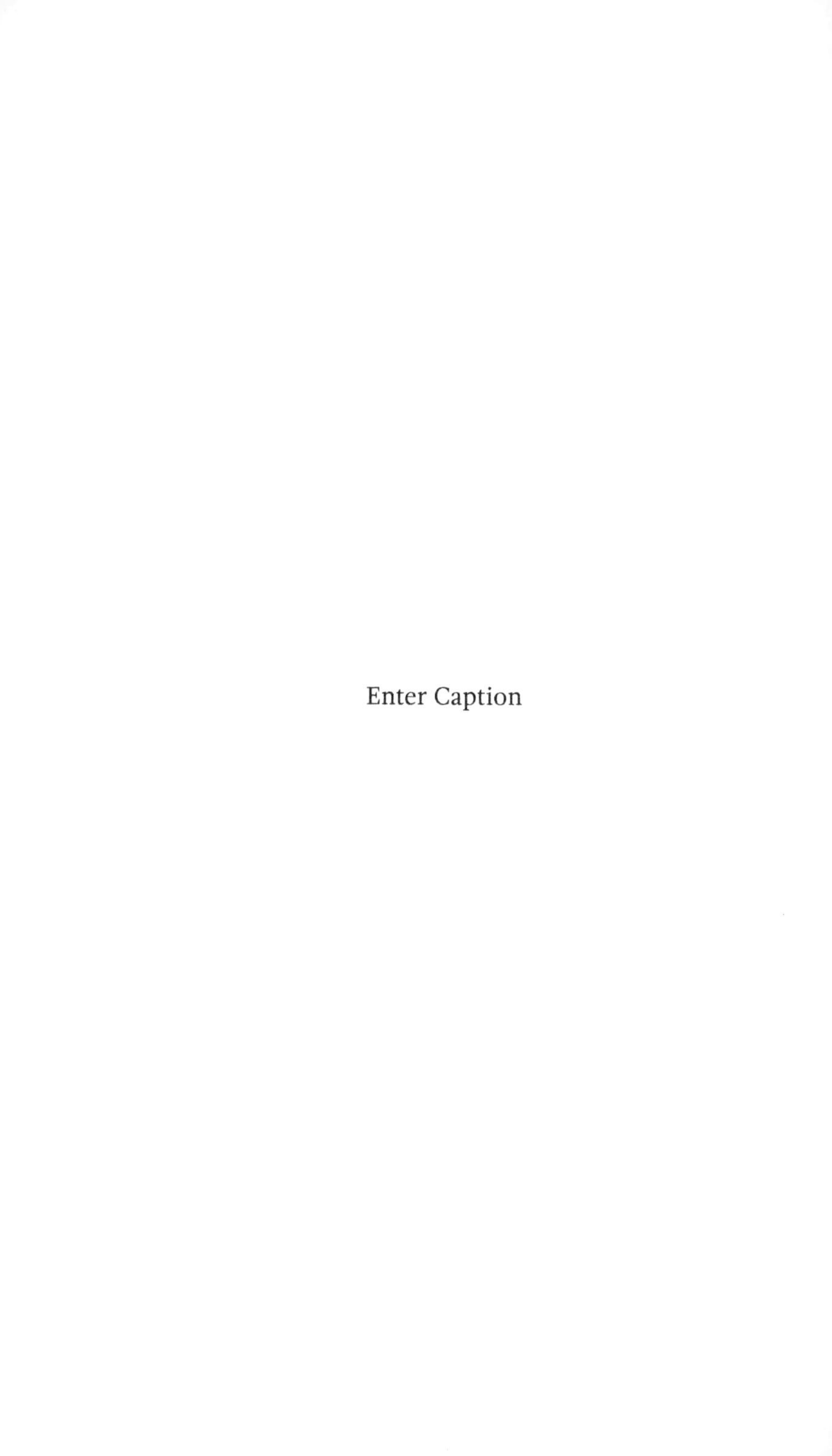
Enter Caption

CHAPTER THIRTY-TWO

INTRODUCTION TO THE PROFIT FIRST SYSTEM

Profit First is a revolutionary financial management system that aims to help businesses achieve long-term financial stability and profitability by flipping the traditional accounting formula on its head. Instead of the conventional approach of Sales - Expenses = Profit, Profit First adheres to the formula of Sales - Profit = Expenses. This system was created by successful entrepreneur and author Mike Michalowicz, who himself had struggled with financial management in his early business ventures.

Mike Michalowicz, the creator of Profit First, is a well-known author and speaker in the entrepreneurial community. His previous books, such as "The Pumpkin Plan" and "The Toilet Paper Entrepreneur," have been highly acclaimed for their practical wisdom and actionable advice for small business owners. Mike's personal experiences with financial challenges in his own businesses led him to develop the Profit First system, which he describes as a simple but effective approach to managing cash flow and ensuring profitability in any business.

The key principles of Profit First are based on the age-old principle of "pay yourself first." In this case, business owners are encouraged to prioritize profit by setting aside a predetermined percentage of their income as profit before allocating funds for expenses. By making profit a non-negotiable aspect of financial management, business owners can ensure that they are consistently building wealth and securing the financial future of their business.

One of the main differences between Profit First and traditional financial management strategies is its focus on profit as the ultimate goal. While many businesses operate on the assumption that profit will naturally follow after covering expenses, Profit First encourages businesses to prioritize profit from the outset. This shift in mindset can have profound effects on the financial health of a business and lead to sustainable growth over time.

There are numerous examples of businesses that have successfully implemented the Profit First system and achieved remarkable results. One such example is that of XYZ Company, a small manufacturing business struggling with cash flow issues. By implementing the Profit First system and consistently setting aside profit from each sale, XYZ Company was able to stabilize their cash flow, reduce debt, and increase their overall profitability within a matter of months. This success story is just one of many that demonstrates the power of Profit First in transforming struggling businesses into thriving enterprises.

The benefits of adopting the Profit First system are numerous and far-reaching. By prioritizing profit, businesses can ensure financial stability, growth, and long-term sustainability. The system also provides a clear and straightforward framework for managing cash flow, reducing financial stress, and making informed financial decisions. Additionally, the Profit First eBook offers practical tools, tips, and strategies for implementing the system in any business, regardless of size or industry.

While the benefits of Profit First are undeniable, there are potential challenges and drawbacks that businesses may face when implementing this system. Some common challenges include resistance from employees or partners who may be hesitant to change established financial practices, as well as the need for strict discipline in setting aside profit and managing expenses. To overcome these challenges, businesses should communicate the benefits of Profit First to all stakeholders, provide training and support for implementation, and remain consistent in their commitment to prioritizing profit.

In conclusion, the Profit First system offers a fresh perspective on financial management that can help businesses achieve greater profitability, stability, and growth. By following the principles outlined in this system and implementing the strategies recommended in the accompanying eBook, businesses can transform their financial health and secure a prosperous future. With its focus on profit as a priority, Profit First has the potential to revolutionize the way businesses approach financial management and ultimately lead to greater success and fulfillment for business owners and entrepreneurs alike.

CHAPTER THIRTY-THREE

Understanding the Core Principles of Profit First

In the world of business, maximizing profits is a key goal for every entrepreneur. However, many businesses struggle to maintain healthy cash flow and profitability. This is where the Profit First system comes into play. Developed by Mike Michalowicz, Profit First is a revolutionary financial management system that helps business owners transform their businesses into profitable entities.

The Profit First system is based on four core principles that are designed to change the way you think about money, profits, and financial management. By following these principles, you can take control of your finances, increase profitability, and ensure the long-term success of your business. Let's dive into each of these core principles and understand how they can help you achieve financial success.

1) Pay Yourself First

The first core principle of Profit First is to pay yourself first. This may seem counterintuitive for many business owners, who are used to reinvesting profits back into the business. However, by paying yourself first, you prioritize your own financial well-being and ensure that you are rewarded for your hard work.

To implement this principle, set aside a percentage of your revenue as profit before allocating funds to expenses. This ensures that you are always putting money aside for yourself, rather than relying on what is left over after expenses. By paying yourself first, you create a mindset shift that places your financial security at the forefront of your business operations.

For example, let's say your business generates Rs. 1000000 in revenue each month. If you decide to pay yourself 5% as profit, you would set aside Rs. 50000 each month. This money is yours to keep, allowing you to build personal wealth while running your business.

2) Allocate Money to Different Accounts

The second core principle of Profit First is to allocate money to different accounts based on predetermined percentages. By separating your revenue into different accounts, you can effectively manage cash flow, track expenses, and ensure that funds are allocated to their intended purposes.

To implement this principle, open multiple bank accounts for different purposes, such as profit, owner's compensation, tax savings, and operating expenses. Allocate a certain percentage of your revenue to each account, ensuring that funds are kept separate and never commingled.

For example, if you allocate 50% of your revenue to operating expenses, 5% to profit, 30% to owner's compensation, and 15% to tax savings, you would deposit Rs. 500000 into your operating expenses account, Rs.50000 into your profit account, Rs. 300000 into your owner's compensation account, and Rs. 150000 into your tax savings account if your business generates Rs. 1000000 in revenue.

3) Use Small Plates

The third core principle of Profit First is to use small plates, inspired by the concept of the "envelope system" popularized by Dave Ramsey. By using small plates, you limit the amount of money available for expenses, forcing you to prioritize spending and make strategic financial decisions.

To implement this principle, set a fixed budget for operating expenses and stick to it. By restricting the amount of money available for expenses, you can control costs, eliminate wasteful spending, and improve profitability. This forces you to become more creative and resourceful with your resources, ultimately leading to greater financial discipline.

For example, if you allocate Rs. 500000 for operating expenses each month, you must prioritize spending and make strategic decisions about which expenses are essential and which can be cut back. By using small plates, you limit the amount of money available for expenses, promoting financial discipline and responsible spending.

4) Remove Your Profit

The fourth core principle of Profit First is to remove your profit from your operating account regularly. By removing your profit, you ensure that your hard work is rewarded and that your business is generating sustainable profits. This principle reinforces the importance of paying yourself first and prioritizing your financial well-being.

To implement this principle, transfer your profit percentage from your operating account to your profit account on a regular basis. This ensures that your profit is kept separate from your operating expenses and that it is not used for day-to-day operations. By removing your profit, you create a financial buffer that can be used for personal expenses, investments, or savings.

For example, if you set aside 5% of your revenue as profit and your business generates Rs. 1000000 in revenue each month, you would transfer Rs. 50000 from your operating account to your profit account regularly. This money is yours to keep and can be used for personal expenses, investments, or savings, rewarding you for your hard work and dedication.

In conclusion, the four core principles of Profit First – Pay Yourself First, Allocate Money to Different Accounts, Use Small Plates, and Remove Your Profit – are designed to help business owners take control of their finances and increase profitability. By following these principles and implementing the Profit First system, you can transform your business into a profitable entity, prioritize your financial well-being, and ensure long-term success. Take the first step towards financial freedom and implement the Profit First system in your business today.

CHAPTER THIRTY-FOUR

ASSESSING YOUR CURRENT FINANCIAL SITUATION

As a business owner, one of the most crucial steps in implementing the Profit First system is assessing your current financial situation. This involves taking a close look at your business's financial health, understanding where your money is going, and identifying areas where you can improve profitability. In this chapter, we will guide you through a comprehensive assessment of your financial standing, including reviewing financial statements, identifying key performance indicators, analyzing revenue and expenses, and addressing cash flow challenges.

1. Evaluating Your Current Financial Health

Before you can start implementing the Profit First system, it's important to have a clear understanding of your current financial situation. This involves conducting a thorough assessment of your business's financial standing, including reviewing your balance sheet, income statement, and cash flow statement. These financial statements will provide you with a snapshot of your business's financial health, showing you where your money is coming from and where it's going.

Take the time to review each of these statements carefully and identify any areas of concern. Are you consistently operating at a loss? Are your expenses outpacing your revenue? Are your profit margins lower than you would like? By pinpointing these financial red flags, you can begin to develop strategies to address them and improve your overall financial performance.

2. Identifying Key Performance Indicators

Key performance indicators (KPIs) are metrics that you can use to gauge your business's financial performance. These KPIs can help you track your progress towards your financial goals and identify areas you may need to make adjustments. Examples of financial KPIs include gross profit margin, net profit margin, and return on investment.

By establishing KPIs for your business, you can track your financial performance over time and make informed decisions to improve profitability. For example, if your gross profit margin is lower than industry standards, you may need to reevaluate your pricing strategy or find ways to reduce your cost of goods sold.

3. Analyzing Revenue and Expenses

One of the key aspects of assessing your current financial situation is analyzing your revenue and expenses. This involves looking closely at your income statement to see where your money is coming from and where it's going. By categorizing your revenue and expenses, you can identify areas of overspending or inefficiency and make adjustments to improve your profitability.

For example, if you notice that a significant portion of your expenses is going towards overhead costs, you may need to find ways to reduce these expenses or increase your revenue to offset them. By conducting a detailed analysis of your revenue and expenses, you can identify areas where you can make changes to increase your bottom line.

4. Identifying Profit Leaks

Profit leaks are areas in your business where money is being wasted or spent unnecessarily. These can include excessive overhead, unnecessary expenses, or operational inefficiencies that are eating into your profits. By identifying and plugging these profit leaks, you can optimize your profitability and improve your financial health.

For example, if you notice that you are spending too much on marketing expenses that aren't generating a significant return on investment, you may need to reallocate these funds to more profitable initiatives. By addressing profit leaks in your business, you can increase your bottom line and improve your overall financial performance.

5. Assessing Cash Flow Patterns

Cash flow is the lifeblood of your business, and understanding the flow of cash in and out of your business is essential for financial success. By assessing your cash flow patterns, you can identify opportunities to improve cash flow management, address cash flow challenges, and optimize your profitability.

Take the time to review your cash flow statement and analyze your cash flow patterns. Are you consistently experiencing cash flow shortages? Are there times of the year when your cash flow is particularly tight? By recognizing these patterns, you can develop strategies to improve cash flow management and ensure that your business has enough cash on hand to operate smoothly.

6. Developing Strategies to Improve Financial Performance

Once you have assessed your current financial situation, identified key performance indicators, analyzed revenue and expenses, identified profit leaks, and assessed cash flow patterns, it's time to develop strategies to improve your financial performance. This may involve implementing the Profit First system, adjusting your pricing strategy, reducing expenses, increasing revenue, or finding other ways to optimize profitability.

For example, you may decide to allocate a certain percentage of your revenue to profit and set up separate bank accounts for your profit, owner's pay, taxes, and operating expenses. By implementing the Profit First system, you can ensure that you are consistently setting aside profits for your business and improving your overall financial health.

In conclusion, assessing your current financial situation is a critical step in implementing the Profit First system and improving your business's profitability. By evaluating your financial health, identifying key performance indicators, analyzing revenue and expenses, identifying profit leaks, assessing cash flow patterns, and developing strategies to improve financial performance, you can optimize your profitability and achieve long-term financial success. Use the insights and practical tips provided in this chapter to implement the Profit First system effectively and take control of your business's finances.

CHAPTER THIRTY-FIVE

SETTING UP PROFIT FIRST WITHIN YOUR BUSINESS

Implementing the Profit First system within your business can be a game-changer in terms of managing your finances and increasing profitability. By allocating your income into separate accounts for different purposes, you can ensure that you are always setting aside money for profit, owner's pay, taxes, and operating expenses. In this chapter, we will walk you through the process of setting up the Profit First system within your business.

Assessing the Current Financial Health of Your Business:

Before you can determine how to allocate your income, you need to assess the current financial health of your business. This includes looking at your revenue, expenses, and any outstanding debts. Take a close look at your cash flow to understand how money is flowing in and out of your business. This will help you determine where you can make adjustments to improve your financial situation.

Determining Target Allocation Percentages:

Once you have a clear understanding of your current financial situation, you can determine target allocation percentages for each account. The Profit First system recommends starting with the following percentages:

- Profit: 5-10%
- Owner's Pay: 50%
- Taxes: 15-20%
- Operating Expenses: 30-50%

These percentages can be adjusted based on the unique needs of your business, but they provide a good starting point for most small businesses.

Opening Separate Bank Accounts:

The next step is to open separate bank accounts for each of the accounts you will be allocating money to. This will help you keep your finances organized and ensure that you are always setting aside money for profit, owner's pay, taxes, and operating expenses.

Here is a step-by-step guide on how to open separate bank accounts for each purpose:

1. Research different banks and account options to find the best fit for your business.

2. Contact the bank to set up the new accounts. You may need to provide documentation such as your business license, PAN number, and proof of address.

3. Label each account accordingly (Profit, Owner's Pay, Taxes, Operating Expenses).

4. Set up automatic transfers from your main operating account to each of the designated accounts based on the target allocation percentages you have determined.

Practical Tips and Examples:

- Automate your finances as much as possible to ensure that money is consistently being allocated to each account. This will help you stay on track with your financial goals.

- Monitor your accounts regularly to track your progress and make adjustments as needed. If you notice that one account is consistently low, you may need to adjust your allocation percentages.

- Consider working with a financial advisor or accountant to help you set up the Profit First system and manage your finances effectively.

By following these steps and tips, you can successfully set up the Profit First system within your business and start managing your finances more effectively. By allocating money for profit, owner's pay, taxes, and operating expenses, you can improve profitability and ensure the long-term financial health of your business.

CHAPTER THIRTY-SIX

PRACTICAL TOOLS AND STRATEGIES FOR EFFECTIVE IMPLEMENTATION

One of the key elements of successfully implementing the Profit First in your business is creating a Profit First. This involves determining your revenue targets, setting up different bank accounts for each of the Profit First categories (Profit, Owner's Pay, Taxes, and Operating Expenses), and implementing a specific rhythm for allocating funds to these accounts.

To start, you'll first need to establish your revenue targets based on your current financial situation and goals. This involves analyzing your historical financial data, identifying areas for improvement, and setting realistic revenue goals for each category. Once you have a clear understanding of your revenue targets, you can then allocate percentages of your revenue to each of the Profit First categories.

After determining your revenue allocations, the next step is to set up separate bank accounts for each of the Profit First categories. This allows you to visually see the distribution of funds and prevents you from dipping into funds designated for other purposes. It's essential to keep these accounts separate to ensure that you stick to your budget and maintain financial discipline.

Once you have your accounts set up, the next step is to establish a rhythm for allocating funds to each account. This can be done on a bi-weekly or monthly basis, depending on your cash flow and financial needs. A common approach is to allocate funds to the Profit account first, followed by Owner's Pay, Taxes, and Operating Expenses. By implementing a regular rhythm for allocating funds, you can ensure that you prioritize your profits and maintain financial stability.

Setting up automatic transfers and allocations is another crucial step in implementing the Profit First system. By automating the process, you can streamline your financial management and ensure that funds are allocated to the appropriate accounts without any additional effort on your part. This can be done through your bank's online banking system or by using financial management software that allows for automated transfers.

In addition to setting up automatic transfers, it's important to regularly monitor your financial data and adjust your allocations as needed. This involves tracking your revenue, expenses, and cash flow on a regular basis to ensure that you are staying on track with your Profit First budget. By reviewing your financial data regularly, you can identify any areas of improvement or potential challenges and make adjustments accordingly.

To help you confidently implement the Profit First system in your business, here are some tips for success:

1. Start small and gradually increase your allocations over time. It's okay to start with conservative percentages and adjust as needed based on your financial performance.

2. Communicate your Profit First budget with your team and involve them in the process. By getting buy-in from your team, you can ensure that everyone is on board with the new financial management system.

3. Seek professional guidance if needed. If you are unsure about how to set up your Profit First budget or encounter any challenges along the way, consider working with a financial advisor or accountant who is familiar with the Profit First system.

4. Stay disciplined and committed to your Profit First budget. It may take some time to adjust to the new system, but by staying consistent and following the established rhythm, you can start to see the benefits of prioritizing profits in your business.

By following these practical tools and strategies for effective implementation, you can confidently implement the Profit First system in your business and start to see improvements in your financial health and profitability. With careful planning, regular monitoring, and a commitment to financial discipline, you can successfully implement the Profit First system and achieve your financial goals.

CHAPTER THIRTY-SEVEN

CASE STUDIES SHOWCASING SUCCESSFUL IMPLEMENTATION

Case Study: Transforming Finances with Profit First System

Before Implementing Profit First System:

Business: Dr. Mehta, a dentist based in Mumbai, India, operated a small dental clinic catering to local residents. Despite a steady stream of patients, Dr. Mehta faced significant challenges in managing the financial aspects of his clinic. He struggled with irregular cash flow, difficulty in covering expenses, and a lack of clarity regarding profitability. This financial uncertainty often led to stress and anxiety, impacting both the operations of the clinic and Dr. Mehta's overall satisfaction with his practice.

Life: The financial challenges Dr. Mehta faced in his clinic spilled over into his personal life. He found it difficult to separate work from home, often spending long hours at the clinic to address financial concerns. This resulted in strained relationships with his family and a decreased sense of fulfillment in his personal life.

Steps Taken to Implement Profit First System:

1. **Education and Training**: Dr. Mehta sought out resources and workshops on financial management for small businesses, where he learned about the Profit First system. He studied the principles outlined in the system and gained an understanding of how to implement them in his dental practice.
2. **Assessment and Analysis**: Dr. Mehta conducted a thorough assessment of his clinic's financial situation. He analyzed his income, expenses, and cash flow patterns to determine the most effective way to implement the Profit First system.
3. **Setting Up Separate Bank Accounts**: Following the guidelines of the Profit First system, Dr. Mehta opened separate bank accounts for profit, taxes, operating expenses, and owner's compensation. This allowed him to allocate funds appropriately and maintain better control over his finances.
4. **Implementation and Adjustment**: Dr. Mehta gradually implemented the Profit First system into his clinic's operations. He monitored his cash flow regularly and made adjustments as needed to ensure that he stayed on track with his profit targets.

Changes and Benefits Realized:

1. **Financial Stability**: Implementing the Profit First system helped Dr. Mehta achieve greater financial stability in his dental clinic. By prioritizing profit and

setting aside funds for taxes and operating expenses, he was better equipped to handle fluctuations in cash flow and unexpected expenses.

2. **Increased Profitability**: With a clearer focus on profit, Dr. Mehta was able to improve the profitability of his clinic. By consistently setting aside a portion of his income as profit, he saw a significant improvement in his bottom line.

3. **Improved Cash Flow Management**: The Profit First system provided Dr. Mehta with better control over his clinic's cash flow. By allocating income to separate bank accounts, he reduced the risk of cash flow shortages and late payments, leading to smoother clinic operations.

4. **Better Work-Life Balance**: With his clinic's finances in order, Dr. Mehta achieved a better work-life balance. He no longer felt overwhelmed by financial stress and was able to spend more quality time with his family outside of work.

5. **Enhanced Overall Well-being**: The reduction in financial stress and improved work-life balance contributed to Dr. Mehta's enhanced overall well-being. He felt happier, more fulfilled, and more confident in both his professional and personal life.

In conclusion, implementing the Profit First system brought about significant positive changes for Dr. Mehta, both in his dental clinic and personal life. By prioritizing profit, managing cash flow effectively, and achieving greater financial clarity, Dr. Mehta was able to build a stronger, more resilient practice while enjoying a higher quality of life.

Case Study: Transforming Finances with Profit First System

Before Implementing Profit First System:

Business: Ms. Sharma operated a small digital marketing agency in Bangalore, India, offering services such as social media management, content creation, and online advertising. Despite having a steady stream of clients, Ms. Sharma struggled with managing the financial aspects of her business effectively. She often found herself facing cash flow shortages, struggling to cover expenses, and unsure about the profitability of her projects. This financial uncertainty led to stress and anxiety, impacting both the operations of the agency and Ms. Sharma's overall satisfaction with her business.

Life: The financial challenges Ms. Sharma faced in her business spilled over into her personal life. She found it difficult to separate work from home, often spending long hours at the agency to address financial concerns. This resulted in strained relationships with her family and friends and a decreased sense of fulfillment in her personal life.

Steps Taken to Implement Profit First System:

1. **Education and Training**: Ms. Sharma sought out resources and workshops on financial management for small businesses, where she learned about the Profit First system. She studied the principles outlined in the system and gained an understanding of how to implement them in her digital marketing agency.

2. **Assessment and Analysis**: Ms. Sharma conducted a thorough assessment of her agency's financial situation. She analyzed her income, expenses, and cash flow patterns to determine the most effective way to implement the Profit First system.

3. **Setting Up Separate Bank Accounts**: Following the guidelines of the Profit First system, Ms. Sharma opened separate bank accounts for profit, taxes, operating expenses, and owner's compensation. This allowed her to allocate funds appropriately and maintain better control over her finances.

4. **Implementation and Adjustment**: Ms. Sharma gradually implemented the Profit First system into her agency's operations. She monitored her cash flow regularly and made adjustments as needed to ensure that she stayed on track with her profit targets.

Changes and Benefits Realized:

1. **Financial Stability**: Implementing the Profit First system helped Ms. Sharma achieve greater financial stability in her digital marketing agency. By prioritizing profit and setting aside funds for taxes and operating expenses, she was better equipped to handle fluctuations in cash flow and unexpected expenses.

2. **Increased Profitability**: With a clearer focus on profit, Ms. Sharma was able to improve the profitability of her agency. By consistently setting aside a portion of her income as profit, she saw a significant improvement in her bottom line.

3. **Improved Cash Flow Management**: The Profit First system provided Ms. Sharma with better control over her agency's cash flow. By allocating income to separate bank accounts, she reduced the risk of cash flow shortages and late payments, leading to smoother agency operations.

4. **Better Work-Life Balance**: With her agency's finances in order, Ms. Sharma achieved a better work-life

balance. She no longer felt overwhelmed by financial stress and was able to spend more quality time with her family and friends outside of work.

5. **Enhanced Overall Well-being**: The reduction in financial stress and improved work-life balance contributed to Ms. Sharma's enhanced overall well-being. She felt happier, more fulfilled, and more confident in both her professional and personal life.

In conclusion, implementing the Profit First system brought about significant positive changes for Ms. Sharma, both in her digital marketing agency and personal life. By prioritizing profit, managing cash flow effectively, and achieving greater financial clarity, Ms. Sharma was able to build a stronger, more resilient business while enjoying a higher quality of life.

CHAPTER THIRTY-EIGHT

MONITORING AND ADJUSTING YOUR PROFIT FIRST SYSTEM

Congratulations on implementing the Profit First system in your business! Now that you have your Profit First accounts set up and are allocating percentages of revenue to each account, it is important to regularly monitor and adjust your system to ensure that it is working effectively for your business. In this chapter, we will discuss how to track financial progress using Profit First, utilize financial reports and metrics to gauge the effectiveness of allocations, interpret key financial reports like balance sheets and income statements, discuss specific metrics relevant to Profit First, identify when adjustments to allocation percentages are necessary, reallocate funds among Profit First accounts in common scenarios, explore long-term sustainability strategies for continued profitability, and the importance of regularly reviewing and refining the Profit

First system to adapt to changes in business and market conditions.

Tracking Financial Progress Using Profit First

One of the key tenets of the Profit First system is regular monitoring of your financial progress. This involves tracking your revenue, expenses, and Profit First account balances on a regular basis. By keeping a close eye on your financial metrics, you can quickly identify any issues or trends that may require adjustments to your allocation percentages.

Utilizing Financial Reports and Metrics

In order to gauge the effectiveness of your Profit First allocations, it is essential to utilize financial reports and metrics to track your business's financial health. Key reports such as balance sheets and income statements can provide valuable insights into your business's profitability and cash flow. By analyzing these reports on a regular basis, you can identify areas where adjustments may need to be made to your allocation percentages.

Interpreting Key Financial Reports

Balance sheets and income statements are two of the most important financial reports for business owners to analyze. A balance sheet provides a snapshot of your business's financial position at a specific point in time, showing your assets, liabilities, and equity. An income statement, on the other hand, shows your business's revenue, expenses, and profit or loss over a period of time. By understanding how to interpret these reports, you can make informed decisions about how to adjust your Profit First allocations to improve your business's financial health.

Specific Metrics Relevant to Profit First

In addition to balance sheets and income statements, there are several key metrics that are particularly relevant to the Profit First system. These metrics include your operating expenses as a percentage of revenue, your gross profit margin, and your net profit margin. By tracking these metrics, you can gain valuable insights into your business's financial performance and make informed decisions about adjusting your allocation percentages.

Scaling Your Business with Profit First

Identifying When Adjustments are Necessary

There are several scenarios in which adjustments to your Profit First allocation percentages may be necessary. For example, if your operating expenses are consistently higher than the recommended percentage, you may need to reduce your expenses or increase your revenue in order to maintain profitability. Similarly, if your profit margins are lower than desired, you may need to adjust your allocation percentages to ensure that you are setting aside enough profit for your business.

Reallocating Funds Among Profit First Accounts

In some cases, you may need to reallocate funds among your Profit First accounts in order to address specific financial challenges. For example, if your tax account is consistently underfunded, you may need to allocate a higher percentage of revenue to this account in order to ensure that you have enough set aside for tax payments. By regularly reviewing your Profit First accounts and making adjustments as needed, you can ensure that your business's financial needs are being met.

Long-Term Sustainability Strategies

In order to ensure the long-term sustainability of your Profit First system, it is important to regularly review and refine your allocations to adapt to changes in your business and market conditions. By staying on top of your financial reports, tracking key metrics, and making adjustments as necessary, you can position your business for continued profitability and success.

Regular Review and Refinement

Finally, it is essential to regularly review and refine your Profit First system in order to ensure that it remains effective for your business. This may involve periodically revisiting your allocation percentages, analyzing your financial reports, and making adjustments as needed to address any financial challenges that arise. By staying proactive and attentive to your business's financial health, you can maintain a strong Profit First system that supports your long-term success.

In conclusion, monitoring and adjusting your Profit First system is essential for the success of your business. By tracking financial progress, utilizing financial reports and metrics, interpreting key financial reports, identifying when adjustments are necessary, reallocating funds among Profit First accounts, exploring long-term sustainability strategies, and regularly reviewing and refining your system, you can ensure that your business remains profitable and financially healthy. Remember, Profit First is a dynamic system that requires regular attention and adjustment to meet your business's evolving needs. By staying proactive and committed to your financial goals, you can achieve sustainable profitability and long-term success.

CHAPTER THIRTY-NINE

Overcoming Common Challenges in Implementing Profit First

Congratulations on taking the first step towards implementing the Profit First system in your business! As with any new system or process, there may be challenges that arise along the way. In this chapter, we will address common roadblocks that entrepreneurs encounter when implementing Profit First and provide practical tips and strategies for overcoming them. We will also discuss effective strategies for staying on track with allocations and how to handle unexpected financial challenges while following the Profit First system.

Common Challenges and How to Overcome Them:

1. Lack of Discipline: One of the most common challenges when implementing Profit First is maintaining discipline with your allocations. It can be tempting to dip into your profit or tax accounts for other expenses, especially when cash flow is tight. To overcome this challenge, it's essential to create a separate bank account for each allocation and automate transfers on payday. This way, the money is out of sight, out of mind, and you are less likely to touch it.

Real-Life Example: Sarah, a small business owner, struggled with discipline when it came to her profit account. She would often transfer money back into her operating account to cover unexpected expenses. However, once she automated transfers and set up separate bank accounts for each allocation, she was able to resist the temptation to dip into her profit account.

2. Insufficient Cash Flow: Another common challenge is having insufficient cash flow to meet all your expenses and still allocate funds to profit, taxes, and other accounts. To overcome this challenge, focus on increasing revenue by finding new streams of income, cutting unnecessary expenses, and improving operational efficiency. It may also be helpful to adjust your allocation percentages based on your current financial situation.

Case Study: Mark, a service-based business owner, was struggling to allocate funds to his profit account due to low cash flow. By increasing his prices, optimizing his pricing structure, and reducing non-essential expenses, he was able to generate more revenue and consistently allocate funds to all his accounts.

3. Unexpected Financial Challenges: Unexpected financial challenges, such as a major client not paying on time or a sudden decrease in sales, can disrupt your Profit First system. In these situations, it's important to be flexible and adjust your allocations accordingly. You may need to temporarily pause contributions to your profit or tax accounts to cover essential expenses and weather the storm.

Step-by-Step Guide: In case of unexpected financial challenges, conduct a thorough review of your financial situation and prioritize your expenses. Communicate with your team about the situation and brainstorm creative solutions to generate additional revenue or reduce costs. Remember that temporary adjustments to your allocations are okay as long as you return to your original plan once the situation improves.

Conclusion:

Implementing the Profit First system in your business comes with its challenges, but with the right strategies and mindset, you can overcome them. By maintaining discipline with your allocations, increasing revenue, and being flexible in times of need, you will set yourself up for long-term financial success. Remember that every business is different, so don't be afraid to tailor the Profit First system to fit your unique circumstances. Stay motivated, stay focused, and watch your profits grow!

CHAPTER FORTY

SCALING YOUR BUSINESS WITH PROFIT FIRST

As a business owner, profitability and sustainable growth are likely top priorities for you. One way to achieve these goals is by implementing the Profit First system, which focuses on allocating funds strategically to support growth initiatives while maintaining profitability. In this chapter, we will discuss how to leverage Profit First to support the growth of your business effectively.

Implementing Profit First to Facilitate Sustainable Business Growth:

The first step to leveraging Profit First to support the growth of your business is to set up proper cash flow management systems. By allocating funds to different bank accounts based on Profit First principles (Profit, Owner's Pay, Taxes, Operating Expenses), you can ensure that your business is always running in a profitable manner. This system will also help you prioritize your expenditure and ensure that you are always able to pay yourself and your taxes.

Managing Cash Flow Effectively During Periods of Expansion:

When your business is in a growth phase, it is crucial to manage your cash flow effectively to avoid running into financial difficulties. Profit First can help you control your expenses and allocate funds to different areas of your business strategically. By setting aside a percentage of revenue for profit and taxes, you can ensure that you can cover your expenses and still have funds left over for growth initiatives.

Strategies for Handling Cash Flow Challenges While Scaling the Business:

Scaling a business can often lead to cash flow challenges as expenses increase. To overcome this, it is essential to have a solid cash flow management system in place. Profit First can help you navigate these challenges by providing a clear framework for allocating funds and ensuring that you always have enough cash on hand to support your growth initiatives.

Tips for Allocating Funds Strategically to Support Growth Initiatives and Maintain Profitability:

To support the growth of your business while maintaining profitability, it is essential to allocate funds strategically. This means setting aside a percentage of revenue for profit and taxes, paying yourself a consistent salary, and closely monitoring your expenses. By following the Profit First system, you can ensure that your business is always running in a financially sustainable manner.

Integrating Profit First Principles into Long-Term Financial Planning Strategies:

To set and achieve financial goals for the future, it is important to integrate Profit First principles into your long-term financial planning strategies. By following the Profit First system consistently, you can ensure that your business is always in a profitable position and can support future growth initiatives effectively.

In conclusion, leveraging Profit First to support the growth of your business can help you achieve long-term financial success. By implementing Profit First principles, managing cash flow effectively during periods of expansion, allocating funds strategically, and integrating these principles into your long-term financial planning strategies, you can set and achieve financial goals for the future while scaling your business successfully.

CHAPTER FORTY-ONE

ADVANCED PROFIT FIRST TECHNIQUES

Implementing advanced Profit First techniques can be a game changer for your business, allowing you to maximize profits and navigate challenges such as economic downturns, tax planning, and investments. In this chapter, we will delve into the nuances of advanced Profit First strategies and provide you with the tools and knowledge you need to take your financial management to the next level.

Advanced Allocation Strategies for Maximizing Profits

One of the key principles of Profit First is allocating a percentage of income to different accounts, such as profit, owner's pay, taxes, and operating expenses. While the basic allocation percentages outlined in the Profit First system provide a solid foundation, advanced allocation strategies can help you optimize profit generation based on your specific business goals and financial performance.

To determine the ideal allocation percentages for your business, consider factors such as your revenue goals, profit margins, and operating expenses. For example, if you are looking to increase your profit margins, you may choose to allocate a higher percentage to the profit account and reduce the percentage allocated to operating expenses.

Regularly reviewing and adjusting your allocation percentages is essential to ensure that your financial strategy remains aligned with your business objectives. If you notice that certain accounts are consistently underfunded or overfunded, it may be time to reassess your allocation percentages and make adjustments as needed.

Using Profit First to Navigate Economic Downturns

Economic downturns can pose significant challenges for businesses, but by leveraging Profit First principles, you can weather the storm and emerge stronger on the other side. During periods of economic uncertainty, it is crucial to conserve cash, reduce expenses, and maintain profitability to protect your business from financial instability.

To conserve cash, consider cutting non-essential expenses and renegotiating contracts with vendors to secure more favorable terms. Additionally, reviewing your allocation percentages and reallocating funds to prioritize profit and cash reserves can help you build a financial buffer to withstand economic downturns.

Integrating Profit First with Tax Planning and Business Investments

Incorporating Profit First into your tax planning strategy can help you minimize tax liabilities and optimize your financial performance. By setting aside a percentage of income for taxes and regularly reviewing your tax obligations, you can ensure that you are prepared to meet your tax obligations without compromising your profitability.

Furthermore, using Profit First principles to inform investment decisions can help you maximize returns and grow your business effectively. Whether you are considering investing in new equipment, expanding your operations, or diversifying your portfolio, incorporating Profit First into your investment strategy can help you make informed decisions that align with your financial goals.

Customizing Profit First for Different Business Models and Industries

Profit First is a versatile financial management system that can be customized to suit the unique needs of different business models and industries. Whether you are running a retail store, a service-based business, or an online e-commerce platform, Profit First can be adapted to fit your specific requirements and help you achieve financial success.

To tailor Profit First to your business model, consider factors such as your revenue streams, profit margins, and expenses. By analyzing your financial data and identifying areas for improvement, you can implement Profit First strategies that align with your business objectives and drive profitability.

In conclusion, implementing advanced Profit First techniques can empower you to take control of your finances, navigate economic downturns, minimize tax liabilities, and make informed investment decisions. By customizing Profit First to suit your business model and industry, you can maximize profitability and achieve long-term financial success.

CHAPTER FORTY-TWO

EPILOGUE: THE RETURN OF THE WISE KING

As we close this journey through the fusion of Chanakya's timeless sutras and the modern Profit Maximiser cash flow system, we come full circle—not as novices seeking answers, but as **leaders equipped with clarity, courage, and conviction.**

Chanakya did not write for merchants. He wrote for kings. But in today's world, every entrepreneur is a king or queen—**ruling over a kingdom called their business.** Like any wise monarch, the key to longevity lies not in flashy declarations or momentary victories, but in:

- Establishing enduring systems.
- Making values-driven decisions.
- Guarding the treasury with precision.
- Serving the people they lead.

You now hold the teachings to not just earn wealth, but to **own, protect, and expand it**—in a way that creates peace, purpose, and prosperity.

This is your time. Your dharma. Your financial legacy to build.

Start where you are. Use what you have. Lead with wisdom. Act with speed. And never forget: **wealth flows to those who are disciplined, not distracted.**

The throne is yours. Rule well.

Bonus Toolkit: Your Chanakya+Profit Maximiser Implementation Planner

Here's a practical toolkit to translate every principle into action.

1. The 4-Account Setup

- **Profit Account** – Begin with 1–5% of all revenue.
- **Owner's Pay Account** – Start with 20–35%.
- **Tax Account** – Allocate 15–20%.
- **OPEX Account** – Operate within what remains.

2. Bi-Monthly Ritual Checklist

- On the 10th and 25th of each month:

  - Allocate income into 4 accounts.
  - Transfer profits to a hidden vault.
  - Review OPEX vs revenue trend.

3. Quarterly Review Template

- What's working?
- What needs optimization?
- How much profit is accumulated?

- Are you tracking toward your Wealth Dharma?

4. Wealth Dharma Statement Prompt
"I use my wealth to..."
Complete the sentence. Print it. Read it monthly.

5. Emergency Buffer Goal

- Business Emergency Fund = 3–6 months OPEX.
- Personal Emergency Fund = 6 months family expenses.

6. Legacy Actions Checklist

- Donate 5–10% of quarterly profit to causes that align with your values.
- Mentor a young entrepreneur.
- Move 25% of annual profit into personal wealth or long-term assets.

7. Commitment Reminders

- "Dridh Sankalpah Lakshya Siddhi" – Discipline > Intelligence.
- "Shubhasya Sheeghram" – Act on clarity quickly.
- "Sampadam Sahanubhuti Karyam" – Wealth must serve.

Use this toolkit as your personal governance manual.

When you lead like Chanakya, wealth follows—not as a chase, but as a consequence.

www.ingramcontent.com/pod-product-compliance
Lightning Source LLC
Chambersburg PA
CBHW042058150726
48005CB00032B/1163